The New York Times

CROSSWORDS TO START YOUR DAY

The New York Times

CROSSWORDS TO START YOUR DAY
75 Easy to Hard Puzzles

Edited by Will Shortz

ST. MARTIN'S GRIFFIN NEW YORK

THE NEW YORK TIMES CROSSWORDS TO START YOUR DAY.

Printed in the United States of America. For information, address
St. Martin's Press, 175 Fifth Avenue, New York, N.Y. 10010.

www.stmartins.com

ISBN 978-1-250-04919-3

St. Martin's Griffin books may be purchased for educational, business, or promotional use.
For information on bulk purchases, please contact Macmillan Corporate and Premium Sales
Department at 1-800-221-7945, extension 5442, or write
specialmarkets@macmillan.com.

First Edition: June 2014

10 9 8 7 6 5 4 3 2 1

EASY 1

ACROSS

1 Concealed
4 It's wide in a May-December romance
10 Quaint words of worry
14 "I love," to Ovid
15 Elaborate architectural style
16 Mineral in thin sheets
17 With 62-Across, question in a children's song
20 Seoul's land
21 Yoko who loved John
22 Hellish suffering
23 Yukon S.U.V. maker
25 Justice Sotomayor
27 Entertain in a festive manner
30 *It's a happening place
34 *Sophocles tragedy
37 Ram's mate
38 Rants
39 Action before crying "You're it!"
40 Full political assemblies
42 Summer: Fr.
43 *British luxury S.U.V.
45 *Star-making title role for Mel Gibson
48 Oozed
49 ___ the Cow (Borden symbol)
52 TV forensic series
53 Old Olds model
56 TiVo, for one
58 Words often after the lowest-priced in a series of items
62 See 17-Across
65 Sorority's counterpart, for short
66 Infuse with oxygen
67 Extra periods of play, in brief
68 1970s–'80s sitcom diner
69 Secret get-togethers
70 Oink : pig :: ___ : cow

DOWN

1 Dove's opposite
2 "If you ask me," in chat rooms
3 Thinker's counterpart
4 Localized charts
5 Liquidy gunk
6 Verbal feedback?
7 Fancy dresses
8 Sneezer's sound
9 "The Raven" writer
10 Pricey watches
11 Song syllables before "It's off to work we go"
12 Thom ___ shoes
13 "Duck soup"
18 Jackson a k a Mr. October
19 Reason for a game delay
24 Gulager of "The Last Picture Show"
26 Veto
27 Rodeo rope
28 Sidled (along)
29 "Cómo ___ usted?"
31 "Pet" annoyance
32 Possessed
33 Tiny bit of crying
34 City near Provo
35 Managed
36 Messy Halloween missiles
40 Forewarns
41 Cantering
43 Doc's written orders
44 Common Market inits.
46 Scouts earn them
47 Tons
50 Aesop's grasshopper, for one
51 The "E" in EGBDF
53 Having two bands, as most radios
54 Apollo plucked it
55 Airline to Israel
57 Food label figs.
59 "Indiana Jones and the Temple of ___"
60 "Do ___ others as . . ."
61 Cuban money
63 Tit for ___
64 Giant among baseball's Giants

by Ed Sessa

2 EASY

ACROSS

1 "Ad ___ per aspera" (Kansas' motto)
6 Fine pillow stuffing
11 Car with a checkered past?
14 Turkish money
15 Parkinson's treatment
16 Egg: Prefix
17 Audibly shocked
18 Military muscle
20 Sign of change at the Vatican
22 Prell rival
23 Ogle
24 Ship slip
25 RR stop
26 Chief Norse god
28 Saffron and ginger
32 Functional lawn adornment
36 Per person
37 Word that can follow both halves of 18-, 20-, 32-, 40-, 54- and 57-Across
39 Plus
40 Take every last cent of
42 Inflatable safety device
44 Curt denial
45 10 Downing St. residents
46 Scoring 100 on
49 Mounted police officer
53 Fade
54 "Go" signal
57 Using all of a gym, as in basketball
59 Eagle's home
60 Network that aired "Monk"
61 007, for one
62 News that may be illustrated by a graph
63 Fictional detective ___ Archer
64 Like the north side of some rocks
65 ___ Park, Colo.

DOWN

1 "There oughta be ___!"
2 "Alas" and "ah"
3 Curly hair or hazel eyes
4 Haile Selassie disciple
5 Bad-mouth
6 Actress Jenna of "Dharma & Greg"
7 Moron
8 Almost any character on "The Big Bang Theory"
9 Fencing blade
10 Radio format
11 Shrink in fear
12 Deflect
13 Word with canal or control
19 Place to get free screwdrivers, say
21 Free throw, e.g.
24 Say, as "adieu"
26 "___ for octopus"
27 "Yeah, like you have a chance!"
28 Regulatory inits. since 1934
29 ___ around with
30 Winter driving hazard
31 Wide strait
32 Word of qualification
33 Priest's garment
34 Org. with a prohibited-items list
35 Sharer's opposite
38 Parisian assent
41 Yule libation
43 Quarantine
45 & 46 Quite bad
47 Effect's partner
48 Something acquired by marriage?
49 Shore fliers
50 Shore fixtures
51 "Snowy" wader
52 ___ Valley, German wine region
54 ___ girl
55 Regrets
56 Senators Cruz and Kennedy
58 Machine part

by Robert Cirillo

ACROSS

1 Tree with acorns
4 Garment under a blouse
7 Expresses derision
13 "___ Mir Bist Du Schön" (1938 hit)
14 Dress that covers the ankles
16 Lassie, for one
17 ___ and tonic
18 Droop in the heat
19 Set off from the margin
20 Lead-in to Bear or Berra
22 Post-monologue spot for Jay Leno
24 Male and female
25 Shade of meaning
27 Diatribes
29 German coal region
30 Former penitentiary in San Francisco Bay
34 "___ luck!"
36 Japanese camera
37 Anger
38 One with a leading role?
39 Santa ___ winds
40 Tex-Mex fare with shells
42 East Lansing sch.
43 Get access, as to a protected site
45 "___ the Sheriff" (Eric Clapton #1 hit)
46 Grated cheese
48 Ancient Peruvian
49 In the midst of
50 "Oh my stars!"
53 Miata maker
56 Prefix with present
58 BlackBerrys and Palms, for short
59 Mark that might be left with greasy fingers
61 Supply-and-demand subj.
63 Monthly entry on a bank statement: Abbr.
64 Say O.K., begrudgingly
65 Western mil. alliance
66 Wedding words
67 Dried plums
68 Imbecile
69 Prankster

DOWN

1 Maternity ward doc
2 Group to which "Y" is sometimes added
3 "Monty Python and the Holy Grail" protagonist
4 Mini Cooper maker
5 Oakland N.F.L.'er
6 Wheel turner
7 Astron., e.g.
8 Eponym of the city now known as Istanbul
9 Like St. Augustine vis-à-vis all U.S. cities
10 Show off at Muscle Beach
11 Alternative to a jail sentence
12 Tennis units
15 Camp classic by the Weather Girls . . . or a homophonic hint to 3-, 8-, 26- and 31-Down
21 Occupied, as a bathroom
23 Alpo alternative
26 So-called "Father of Europe"
28 Sgt., e.g.
31 Shakespeare play that begins "Now is the winter of our discontent"
32 Suffix with buck
33 Joie de vivre
34 "One ___ or two?"
35 Greece's Mount ___
36 1998 Winter Olympics host
41 Musical alternative to BMI
44 Bear: Sp.
47 Infuriate
48 Imbeciles
51 Bit of candy that "melts in your mouth, not in your hand"
52 Legally prevent
53 Car showroom sticker inits.
54 The "A" in U.S.A.: Abbr.
55 South African native
57 Sweet 16 org.
60 Many "Star Trek" extras, for short
62 1, 2, 3, etc.: Abbr.

by John Lieb

4 EASY

ACROSS

1 Fed. procurement overseer
4 Boito's "Mefistofele," e.g.
9 "Delta of Venus" author Nin
14 Giver of a hoot
15 Remove, as a spill
16 Bendel of fashion
17 *Migratory flock
19 Couldn't stand
20 Small French case
21 Appear
22 Plenteous
23 Cuckoo in the head
25 Dada pioneer
28 Heart
29 Greek letter traditionally associated with Earth Day
30 *Singer Amy with six Grammys
33 Drought ender
35 Group of papers
36 *Pegasus, notably
39 Asian capital that was from 2004–07 home of the world's tallest building
41 ___ Minor
42 *"Regardless of the outcome . . ."
44 News items often written years in advance
49 Directional suffix
50 D.C. V.I.P.
51 Dim sum dish
52 Yale Whale players
54 Blarney Stone home
57 Stat for A-Rod
58 Take care of a fly?
60 Witticism . . . or, literally, a description of the answer to each of the four starred clues?
62 Año's start
63 Facing the pitcher
64 Who said "The revolution is not an apple that falls when it is ripe. You have to make it fall"
65 "Hollywood Nights" singer Bob
66 Bronx Bombers
67 Le Mans race unit: Abbr.

DOWN

1 Head toward the setting sun
2 Trade, as places
3 Attraction
4 "Yipe!," online
5 Wordsworth words
6 Sporting weapon
7 Artifice
8 Hypothetical primate
9 "Yes . . . that's the spot . . . yes!"
10 Approaching
11 Like a "Better active today than radioactive tomorrow" sentiment
12 "You can't make me!"
13 Not the main action
18 Course-altering plan?
24 Brothers of old Hollywood
26 Auto take-backs
27 Mummy, maybe
30 Golfer Michelle
31 River through Pakistan
32 Training acad.
34 Like a ballerina
36 Manitoba's capital
37 Big W.S.J. news
38 Charlemagne's domain: Abbr.
39 Plucks, as brows
40 Fleet operator
43 Like a relationship with a narcissist
45 Historical subject for Gore Vidal
46 "It's me again"
47 Chinese martial art
48 Onetime colleague of Ebert
51 "___ Previews" (onetime show of 48-Down)
53 Not doubting
55 Journalist Skeeter of the Harry Potter books
56 Amazon.com ID
59 ___ favor
61 Amt. to the right of a decimal point

by Paula Gamache

EASY 5

ACROSS

1 Big first for a baby
5 Orange tubers
9 Woodworking tools
14 Bistro
15 The "U" of "Law & Order: SVU"
16 Place for a watch
17 Something smashed by Abraham, in Jewish tradition
18 Viral phenomenon
19 New Hampshire's "Live Free or Die," e.g.
20 E. M. Forster novel
23 Glimpse
24 Pepsi ___, sugar-free cola
25 Sicilian secret society
27 Farming: Prefix
30 Growth on old bread
34 Part of the Justice Dept. that conducts raids
35 Peruse again
37 Chips ___! (cookie brand)
38 "Count on me"
41 Challenge
42 Enclosed body of water on a tropical island
43 Harper ___, author of "To Kill a Mockingbird"
44 Mexican miss: Abbr.
45 Fe, chemically
46 Bottomless void
48 General on a Chinese menu
50 Bridge
51 Signature song for MC Hammer
58 Bulgaria's capital
59 Symbol in the center of a Scrabble board
60 Turkish title
62 Yellowstone and Yosemite
63 Limping, say
64 Breakfast chain, briefly
65 Wade noisily
66 "Now I get it"
67 Call it a day

DOWN

1 Biol. or chem.
2 "Look what I did!"
3 Grade meaning "Maybe you failed, but at least you tried"
4 Nancy of the House of Representatives
5 Scrumptious
6 All over again
7 "La Bohème" heroine
8 "Leave in," to a proofreader
9 "This is the worst!"
10 Sent up the wall
11 Penne alternative
12 Villa d'___
13 Put in the overhead bin, say
21 Pictures that can make you dizzy
22 Jinx
25 Some motel employees
26 Fighting (with)
27 Toward the back
28 Beginning, informally
29 Synthetic silk
31 Carol with the words "hear the angel voices"
32 Home Depot rival
33 Units of force
36 Mama Cass
39 Tidy types
40 Not fitting
47 Believers in the essential worth of all religions
49 Secret supply
50 Film ogre voiced by Mike Myers
51 Mail letters?
52 Unwanted stocking stuffer
53 Hairdo for Jimi Hendrix
54 Norway's capital
55 Great Salt Lake state
56 Hunter's garb, for short
57 "Go on, git!"
61 Words With Friends, e.g.

by Joel Fagliano

6 EASY

ACROSS

1 Scolding, nagging sort
6 Hence
10 The opposition
14 John who wrote "Appointment in Samarra"
15 Invitation sender
16 Vagrant
17 See 40-/42-Across
19 Key of Haydn's Symphony No. 12 or 29
20 Refuse
21 Word after sports or training
22 Dummy
23 Seven-time All-Star Sammy
25 Cop's target
27 The "A" of B.A.
31 Latvia neighbor: Abbr.
33 Contemporary of Gandhi
36 Hellmann's product, informally
37 Urge strongly
39 Quaker cereal brand
40 & 42 Subject of the poem that contains the line 17-/65-Across
44 N.E.A. concern
45 Depth charge, in slang
47 Collecting a pension: Abbr.
48 Bakery and pharmacy
50 Story that goes on and on
51 It is, in Ibiza
52 Flutters, as eyelashes
54 Indecent
56 Smart-mouthed
58 Down a sub, e.g.
60 One of the ABC islands
64 Eastern nurse
65 See 40-/42-Across
68 Texter's disclaimer
69 Branch of engineering: Abbr.
70 Tribe with a lake named after it
71 Colors
72 Long hallway effect
73 "This looks bad!"

DOWN

1 First word of "Blowin' in the Wind"
2 Cries of discovery
3 Pro ___
4 Mice, to cats
5 Elaborate stories
6 "___ Crossroads" (1996 Grammy-winning rap song)
7 Relaxing conclusion to a long, hard day
8 Manipulator
9 Rein, e.g.
10 "And ___ off!"
11 Read and blew, for red and blue
12 Fortune 500 company founded in 1995
13 Austin Powers's power
18 Some winter garments
24 Trivial Pursuit wedges, e.g.
26 ___'acte
27 Gather over time
28 Dressing choice
29 Astronomer who coined the word "nova"
30 "___ hear"
32 Show of respect
34 Butler of "Gone With the Wind"
35 Nutritional fig.
38 Fled
41 Bridge position
43 Tick off
46 West Coast engineering institution, informally
49 Pity
53 Note accompanying an F, maybe
55 BBC sci-fi show
56 Invoice stamp
57 Cousin of a Golden Globe
59 With: Fr.
61 "Ain't gonna happen!"
62 Arctic Ocean sighting
63 Suffix with buck
66 Sigma preceder
67 Conclusion

by Jeff Chen

ACROSS

1 Judge's garment
5 Plant with fronds
9 Book after Jonah
14 Zenith
15 Et ___ (and others)
16 Machine at a construction site
17 Lofty
18 Last ones in the pool, say
20 Chicago Cubs spring training site
22 Hosp. areas for accident victims
23 Actress Thurman
24 Pattern for many 1960s T-shirts
26 "Rag Mop" hitmakers, 1950
32 Prefix with task
33 Unmannered sort
34 Lawbreaker, in police lingo
38 E.P.A.-proscribed compound, for short
39 New Jersey's capital
42 Menagerie
43 Hoax
45 Bone: Prefix
46 Chinese or Japanese
48 You've heard it many times before
51 1986 Tom Cruise/ Val Kilmer action film
54 ___ de Cologne
55 "You ___ what you eat"
56 Metal-joining technique
63 Salon
65 Clothes presser
66 Philosopher John who posited a theory of social contract
67 Unabridged dictionary, e.g.
68 Mrs. Charlie Chaplin
69 White from fright, say
70 Library ID
71 Flat-bottomed boat

DOWN

1 Chicago mayor Emanuel
2 "The Andy Griffith Show" boy
3 Panhandles
4 Deplete
5 ___, Straus and Giroux (book publisher)
6 "The Time Machine" people
7 "Puttin' on the ___"
8 Western mil. alliance
9 QB Steve who won a Payton Award
10 Fury
11 Like animals in a 42-Across
12 Furious
13 Hermann who wrote "Steppenwolf"
19 Intestinal prefix
21 Circumference
25 Mind reader's ability, briefly
26 Concert blasters
27 "Thank you very ___"
28 Exile isle for Napoleon
29 Seriously overweight
30 Kemo Sabe's sidekick
31 Equivalent of five houses in Monopoly
35 Basso Pinza
36 Lion's sound
37 Smallish equine
40 McCain : 2008 :: ___ : 2012
41 ___ decongestant
44 Where the Knicks play in N.Y.C.
47 Small apartments
49 Jane who wrote "Pride and Prejudice"
50 Become more intense
51 Small Indian drum
52 Nabisco cookies
53 Fruit with a pit
57 Italian wine area
58 Conductance units
59 Where a baby develops
60 Camaro ___-Z
61 Something you might get your hand slapped for doing
62 Chew like a beaver
64 Luau instrument, informally

by Allan E. Parrish

8 EASY

ACROSS

1 Locales for "Ocean's Eleven" and several Bond films
8 Beirut's land
15 Thousands of fans might do it
16 Japanese art form
17 Unwrap in a hurry
18 Who, What and I Don't Know, in Abbott and Costello's "Who's on First?" routine
19 Neither's partner
20 Abnormal part of Voldemort's visage
21 Concern of Freud
22 Layer of the earth between the crust and the core
25 "Just ___!" ("Be right there!")
26 Marx's "___ Kapital"
27 Hotel amenity often near the elevator
28 Make, as an income
30 Sun
32 Hawaiian garland
33 Suffix with neur-
34 Destruction
37 Talk show host DeGeneres
39 Olive ___ (Popeye's gal)
41 Pool measurement
42 X-ray units
43 Refuse
45 Golf standard
46 13-digit library info
49 Horse color
50 Day before
51 Civil War side: Abbr.
53 Sushi ingredient
55 Sealed, as a driveway
57 Thanksgiving staple
58 "Don't have ___, man!"
59 Thurman of "Pulp Fiction"
60 Napped
62 Grand Canyon locale
66 A lifeguard's whistle might create one
67 Alternative to a forward pass
68 Cowboy seats
69 Pinto and Flounder, in "Animal House"

DOWN

1 Middle: Abbr.
2 Yellowfin tuna
3 Aug. follower
4 "You can't make me!"
5 With 41-Down, title teen in a 2004 indie hit
6 Pig out
7 Capitol Hill V.I.P.: Abbr.
8 University of New Mexico team
9 Wipes off
10 Cut in half
11 Ripen
12 Status-seeking sort . . . or a solver of this puzzle, initially?
13 Last Greek letter
14 Boys, in Bogotá
20 Amateur detective in 1967's "The Clue in the Crossword Cipher"
22 Roger Bannister, notably
23 Amtrak high-speed train
24 "Song Sung Blue" singer
29 1983 Duran Duran hit
31 Ginger ___
35 Ward (off)
36 Destroy, as documents
38 Suffix with shepherd
40 Virgo preceder
41 See 5-Down
44 Undyed
47 South America's largest country
48 Christianity's ___ Creed
51 Anatomical sacs
52 Yemen's capital
54 Secret writings
56 Demolished
61 Antiquated
62 Austrian peak
63 Alternative to .com
64 Scottish denial
65 Franken and Gore

by John Lieb

ACROSS

1 Digital readout, in short
4 So-called "Crime Dog" of public service ads
11 Emergency PC key
14 Debtor's note
15 Certain spray can
16 1960s chess champ Mikhail
17 "De-e-elicious!"
18 Caribbean resort island
20 2008 Tina Fey/Amy Poehler comedy
22 Yale students
23 ___ good deed
24 ___ Day (third Mon. in January)
26 Divas' solos
27 Creature that goes "ribbit"
29 Many a 1930s soap opera
31 Piquant triangular snack chip
33 Failure
34 Desert of Chile
36 3-D art project
41 Oomph
42 Place to analyze some crime evidence
43 White House girl
49 Winery tubs
50 ___ Rock (Australian site)
51 Place with thermal waters
52 One of 100 on the Hill: Abbr.
53 Nevada gambling mecca
54 "He's a priest," per Ogden Nash
58 First explorer to sail directly from Europe to India
62 System of connected PCs
63 Optometrist's focus
64 Crunchy bit ground up in pesto
65 "Reeling in the Years" rockers Steely ___
66 Guitar innovator Paul
67 "No challenge"
68 Professional org. ending eight answers in this puzzle

DOWN

1 Arm or leg
2 Unconscious state
3 Stereotypical airhead of old
4 Underground molten rock
5 Michael of "Superbad"
6 Parent's mom, informally
7 President Reagan
8 Amer. money
9 Watch chain
10 Tallahassee's home: Abbr.
11 And others
12 Green eggs and ham purveyor, in "Green Eggs and Ham"
13 Minor-league baseball level
19 German "Mr."
21 Like some meditative exercises
25 Captain ___, legendary pirate
26 Build a new wing, say
27 Org. that approves new pharmaceuticals
28 Go bad
29 Juliet's beau
30 One-named author of "A Dog of Flanders"
32 Snacks at a Spanish bar
35 "Be on the lookout" alerts, for short
37 Entangle, as yarn
38 Hawkeye Pierce's portrayer
39 Welcome ___ (doorstep item)
40 Muscles that benefit from crunches
43 Publisher of Spider-Man and X-Men comics
44 "Yes, captain!"
45 Microscope parts
46 Classic '80s Camaro
47 Orbital high point
48 Tomorrow, in Tijuana
52 Dull blue-gray
55 Birds appearing on Australia's 50 cent coins
56 "Yes, ___" (gent's reply)
57 Actress Paquin
59 Choose (to)
60 Italian "god"
61 12 months: Sp.

by Tim Croce

10 EASY

ACROSS

1 Communication with the hands: Abbr.
4 Three-note chord
9 Thread holder
14 Defiant response to an order
16 Fictional member of the Potawatomi tribe
17 Boxer's asset
18 Some choristers
19 Leave in, as text
20 "Can you explain this?"
22 [not my error]
25 ___ center
26 Rejuvenation location
29 Searcher's query
36 Entrusted to another for safekeeping
38 Road safety org.
39 Dangerous gas
40 Calendario unit
41 Lay in a hammock, say
42 Very light brown
43 Precisely
45 Antsy premeal question
48 Sculler's need
49 A.M.A. members
50 Cooking vessel with handles
52 "Is it any use?"
58 "___ Jury" (Spillane detective novel)
62 It helps a pitcher get a grip
63 Soothing lotion ingredients
66 Rocky ridge
67 Journalism staple
68 Peels
69 "You said it, ___!"
70 Brian of ambient music

DOWN

1 Hole-making tools
2 Opportunity
3 Isolated
4 Old salt
5 Ham on ___
6 "___ Mommy kissing . . ."
7 Author Sholem
8 Qatar's capital
9 One putting on a show
10 One keeping the beat?
11 Airing
12 Oklahoma Indian
13 Red ink amount
15 Superiors to cpls.
21 Singsong syllable
23 "Checkmate!"
24 Abbr. on a receipt
26 Thread holder?
27 Catch illegally
28 "My Dinner With ___"
30 Provide with a fund
31 Marie Antoinette, par exemple
32 Online time stamp
33 Mississippi's ___ River
34 Black Sea port, to locals
35 One may be above a bucket
37 Media-friendly quote
41 Actor Jared
44 Cry to a plow horse
46 Pilotless planes
47 Right, on a German compass
51 Chicken ___
52 Tinfoil, e.g.
53 Bar mitzvah dance
54 North Sea feeder
55 Bowlers and skimmers
56 K–12, in education
57 Some deer
59 Peach or beech
60 Goldie of "Laugh-In"
61 "Put a tiger in your tank" brand
64 Little wriggler
65 Routing word

by Patrick McIntyre

ACROSS

1 Accomplished
4 Greeted at the door
9 Davis of "A League of Their Own"
14 Academic email address ender
15 Speak grandly
16 Director Welles
17 Score between birdie and bogey
18 Neat in appearance
20 "Nothing left to say"
22 1950s Ford failures
23 Sharpen
24 Glum
25 "In case it's of interest . . . ," on a memo
26 Tierra ___ Fuego
28 Pan in Chinese cookery
30 "Waiting for ___"
34 Air conditioner meas.
36 "The Tears ___ Clown"
38 Modern film genre with dark themes
40 Crew team implement
41 Clickable address, for short
42 Monterrey gold
43 Suffix with glob
44 Three-dimensional
46 One a woman can't trust
47 "I'm gone"
48 Enthusiastic kids' plea
49 Seek, as permission
51 Oscar winner Brynner
53 Stately 33-Down
55 Letters before an alias
57 Make over
60 Small stock purchase
63 Like a weedy garden
65 Just going through the motions
67 Spanish "huzzah!"
68 Prized violin
69 Signal again, as an actor
70 First of the five W's
71 Gracefully limber
72 Expressed one's disapproval
73 Writer Anaïs

DOWN

1 Swimming pool statistic
2 Boise's state
3 *Band with the 1983 hit "Hungry Like the Wolf"
4 Piglets' mothers
5 Expanses
6 *Washington city near the Oregon border
7 "That's adequate"
8 Below zero: Abbr.
9 *Affectedly virtuous
10 Soil problem
11 Salinger title girl
12 Christmas song
13 No ifs, ___ or buts
19 Wrestling official, briefly
21 Buttonless shirt, informally
27 *Hit song for the Kingsmen with famously unintelligible lyrics
29 *Joke starter
31 Blackjack player's option . . . or a description of the answers to the starred clues?
32 Slick
33 See 53-Across
34 Pear variety
35 Finger food at a fiesta
37 Monk's title
39 The Roaring Twenties, e.g.
45 Last of a dozen
50 Fries lightly
52 Spigoted vessel
54 Any of the Andes: Abbr.
56 "Based on ___ story"
58 Metropolitan region that includes India's capital
59 Old-time music hall
60 Translucent gem
61 Actress Moore of "G.I. Jane"
62 G-rated oath
64 Looked at carefully
66 Obsolescent PC monitor type

by Doug Peterson

12 EASY

ACROSS

1 Native Kiwis
6 Big name in power tools
10 Educated guesses: Abbr.
14 Extra Dry brand
15 A, to Mozart
16 Kind of suit worn by a 21-Down
17 Garbage scow that docked with Mir?
19 It's fit to be tied
20 Swapping out Sheen for Rose?
22 Fall result, maybe
24 "That's all ___ wrote"
25 Actor Brynner
26 What an actor plays
27 Excite, as an appetite
30 Roman encyclopedist who died after the eruption of Vesuvius
32 "What Do You Do With ___ in English?" ("Avenue Q" song)
33 Romanov bigwig
34 "Rocks"
35 Boy Scout's reward for karate expertise?
40 Nintendo console
41 Pepper's partner
42 Sum
44 Nahuatl speaker
47 Case for an ophthalmologist
48 Word before "sum"
49 "I am so stupid!"
50 Move hastily
52 Move aimlessly
54 Caveman's injury after discovering fire?
58 Puerto ___
59 Feeling when one's voodoo doll is poked?
62 Designer Marc
63 Coin of Colombia
64 Jungian archetype
65 Slough off
66 Snare
67 Undergo a chemical transformation

DOWN

1 "No ___!" (Spanish "Uncle!")
2 Dadaist Hans
3 Providing hints of the future
4 Havens who sang at Woodstock
5 Some intellectual property
6 Good Housekeeping emblem
7 Soprano ___ Te Kanawa
8 Consume
9 Bloodletting worm
10 Biblical book once combined with Nehemiah
11 Mrs. Woody Allen
12 1986 Tom Cruise film
13 Like a cold, hard gaze
18 Cold one
21 Cool one, once
22 Garment under a blouse
23 Former Virginia senator Chuck
28 "Bali ___" ("South Pacific" song)
29 Dadaist Max
31 Was in the vanguard
33 Meditative martial art
34 "My goof!"
36 Ram's mate
37 Like the apparel donned in "Deck the Halls"
38 Fragrant white flower
39 Razor feature
43 Palme ___ (Cannes award)
44 Likes a bunch
45 City NE of Geneva
46 "Growing Pains" co-star Alan
47 "Growing Pains" family name
48 V-8, e.g.
51 Like a schlimazel
53 Egypt's Sadat
55 The "G" in EGBDF
56 Toon who plays a baritone sax
57 Feed, as pigs
60 Maker of the Canyon truck
61 Consume

by Dan Feyer

ACROSS

1 Wood for a chest
6 Holy Land
10 TV's Dr. ___
14 Love, Italian-style
15 "Dies ___" (Latin hymn)
16 Gossipy Barrett
17 Unseen purchase
19 Like custard and meringue
20 Writer Wiesel
21 Long, long time
22 – – –
24 Transparent, informally
26 "___ Mio"
27 Greet with a honk
29 Reeves of "The Matrix"
32 Holy wars
35 Drag behind, as a trailer
37 Designer Saint Laurent
38 Made in ___ (garment label)
39 You can't make a silk purse out of it, they say
42 Before, poetically
43 Actress Moore of "Ghost"
45 Tell a whopper
46 Buzz and bleep
48 Daniel who wrote "Robinson Crusoe"
50 Drive-in server
52 How to sign a contract
54 Ambassador's helper
58 Birthplace of St. Francis
60 African antelope
61 Part that wags
62 Big name in crackers
63 Like some wasteful government spending
66 Toward shelter, nautically
67 Asia's diminished ___ Sea
68 John ___ (tractor maker)
69 Physiques
70 Words before and after "or not"
71 Attach, as a button

DOWN

1 Bullfighters wave them
2 Writer Zola
3 Cowherd's stray
4 Short operatic song
5 Stimpy's bud
6 Like some detachable linings
7 What bodybuilders pump
8 Wood for a chest
9 Essentials
10 "Blue Suede Shoes" singer
11 Ecstatic state, informally
12 "Bus Stop" playwright
13 Puts down, as tile
18 Spray can
23 Just fine
25 Mortar troughs
26 Great Plains tribe
28 Floundering
30 Stereotypical techie
31 Applications
32 Naomi or Wynonna of country music
33 "Got it!"
34 Clumsy
36 Laundry basin
40 Lighted part of a candle
41 Part of a plant or tooth
44 Becomes charged, as the atmosphere
47 Stuck, with no way to get down
49 Sue Grafton's "___ for Evidence"
51 Really bug
53 Barely bite, as someone's heels
55 Rod who was a seven-time A.L. batting champ
56 Prefix with -glyphics
57 "The ___ DeGeneres Show"
58 Many an Iraqi
59 Corn Belt tower
60 Seize
64 Spanish gold
65 What TV watchers often zap

by John Lampkin

14 Easy

ACROSS

1 Mr. Spock's rank: Abbr.
5 Rosie of "The Jetsons," for one
10 Compressed video format
14 Lascivious sort
15 Archie's sitcom wife
16 Simon & Garfunkel's "___ Rock"
17 Some Wall St. traders
18 Beef up
19 Shoot with Novocain, say
20 Highland slopes
22 Comb maker
23 Puerto Rico y Cuba
24 He drove the serpents from Ireland, in legend
27 Jethro ___
28 Sold-out sign
29 Medicine-approving org.
32 Painter's support
36 Accustoms
38 Diamond Head setting
39 ___ of Tranquillity
41 Mathematician John who was the subject of "A Beautiful Mind"
42 Marcos of the Philippines
45 Britain's Arthur Wellesley, with "the"
48 Band with the multiplatinum albums "Out of Time" and "Monster"
49 P, to Pythagoras
51 K.G.B. concern
52 Indian pipe player, maybe
57 Uno + cuatro
60 Santa ___ winds
61 Butcher's string
62 Eastern nurse
63 Jeff of the Electric Light Orchestra
65 Drain feature
66 Comb-over's locale
67 Bird feeder fill
68 Malaria symptom
69 Checked out
70 Critical times of attack
71 Count in a weight room

DOWN

1 Cantankerous folks
2 "How Are Things in Glocca ___?" (1947 hit song)
3 Most populous of the United Arab Emirates
4 Like Cain, toward Abel
5 Actor Stephen
6 Strange birds
7 Lavatory fixture
8 Bewhiskered frolickers
9 However, briefly
10 Capital of Belarus
11 Simon of Simon & Garfunkel
12 Actress Stone of "The Help"
13 Chews the fat
21 Double ___ Oreos
23 A browser has one
25 Mideast grp.
26 Red-hot feeling
29 Herr's honey
30 Information ___
31 1980s U.S. Davis Cup captain
32 Evening in Paris
33 Checked in, say
34 [May I have your attention?]
35 Opus ___
37 Drawers in drawers
40 Companion who's a knockout
43 Early Bond foe
44 "Gotcha!"
46 Word before "That's gotta hurt!"
47 GPS above-the-Equator fig.
50 Approved
52 Timetable: Abbr.
53 Nine: Prefix
54 No-see-um
55 Turn out to be
56 Spanish kings
57 South Africa has a famous one
58 Polite words after "if"
59 "Great" detective of children's literature
63 It may be dropped when one trips
64 Hook shape

by Kristian House

ACROSS

1 Pleasant
5 Pretentious
9 Old PC monitors
13 Radio's "___ in the Morning"
14 Lerner's partner in musicals
15 Meat cut that may be "tender"
16 Comedian with a mock 1968 presidential campaign
18 Detroit product
19 Printing units: Abbr.
20 Villain's look
21 Puff piece?
22 "Absolutely!"
23 Money that doesn't completely satisfy a debt
25 ___ and hers
27 Bob Schieffer's network
28 Roman god of love
30 Manufacture
34 Cut off, as a branch
37 Tricky task in a driver's test
40 Kindergartner, e.g.
41 Gents' counterparts
42 Furniture chain founded in Sweden
43 Floppy feature of a dachshund
44 Co. in a 2000 merger that became Verizon
45 Event that might have a pillow fight
52 Stock market debut, for short
55 "La Bohème" or "La Traviata"
56 Psychologist Alfred
57 Wrigley Field player
58 The "I" in M.I.T.: Abbr.
59 Casino cry . . . or a hint for 16-, 23-, 37- and 45-Across
61 Actor Rogen
62 Beethoven dedicatee
63 Job for a barber
64 "___ does it!"
65 A great deal
66 Ward of "CSI: NY"

DOWN

1 A bit cold, as weather
2 Spitting ___
3 Truncates
4 Mentalist's skill, briefly
5 Certain IM user
6 Put back to zero, as a tripmeter
7 Insignificant punk
8 Kyoto currency
9 Alleges
10 Noir's counterpart in roulette
11 Giant in Greek myth
12 Angry bull's sound
14 Moon goddess
17 Snakes along the Nile
21 Modern lead-in to cafe
24 Represent
26 Long-term bank offering, briefly
28 Residence like 2-B or 7-J: Abbr.
29 ___ Zedong
30 Santa ___, Calif.
31 Stoplight color
32 Yale grad
33 King Kong, notably
34 "Whatever!"
35 Number dialed before an area code
36 Augusta National org.
38 Andes animal
39 Do-it-yourselfer's purchase
43 Coarse, as humor
44 Greek street food
45 Sang-froid
46 Sleep problem
47 Remarks not to be taken seriously
48 Renaissance painter Veronese
49 Own up (to)
50 Like non-oyster months
51 Head: Fr.
53 Eliza, to Henry Higgins
54 Illinois senator-turned-president
59 Collectible frame
60 A touchdown is worth six: Abbr.

by Zhouqin Burnikel

16 EASY

ACROSS

1 It has a balance: Abbr.
5 Reverberation
9 ___ lazuli
14 Superdome locale, informally
15 ___ Hubbard, Scientology founder
16 Party or parade
17 Reason for rehab
19 Hardly rambling
20 Give a new title
21 Dutch cheese
23 Six-sided randomizer
24 Two under par
25 Trail
27 New York theater award
29 Plant fungus
30 Darts and snooker
34 Separate into charged particles
37 Actress Gabor
38 Took to the slopes
40 Ref. work that took 70 years to complete
41 Grow fond of
44 Sinatra backers, sometimes
47 Judgment on a book's cover?
49 "Super!"
50 Groundskeeper's bane
53 Pong purveyor
57 "___ out!" (ump's cry)
58 One-billionth of a gig
59 Wild-eyed sort
60 World capital whose name means "victorious"
62 Assortments . . . or what you'll find in 17-, 25-, 30-, 44- and 50-Across?
64 Forest vine
65 Similar
66 Cat or clock preceder
67 Young's partner in accounting
68 Something to avoid
69 Story that can't completely be believed

DOWN

1 Tennis's Agassi
2 Jazz's Chick
3 Adhered (to)
4 Philippine tongue
5 Czech Republic river
6 Grand ___ (vineyard designation)
7 First book of the 12 Minor Prophets
8 Antsy
9 Prisoner's plaint
10 N.Y.C.'s Columbus ___
11 Hell
12 Living ___
13 Fiery horse
18 Organism that splits
22 Condense
25 Onion relative used in soups
26 Babydoll
28 1960 #1 Brenda Lee hit
30 Place to congregate?
31 Thos. Jefferson founded it
32 Conan, for one
33 Close relation, informally
35 Final section of the 40-Across
36 Actors Harris and Helms
39 ___, zwei, drei . . .
42 World Series org.
43 Maritime rescuer
45 Bleated
46 "Good going!"
48 Repeated role for Christian Bale
50 Rinse or spin
51 Show once more
52 Watch with the old slogan "Modern Masters of Time"
54 Singer/songwriter Davis
55 "Got it," in radio lingo
56 "Challenge accepted!"
59 Paradoxical Greek
61 Some pulse takers, for short
63 Mark, as a ballot

by Pete Muller

EASY **17**

ACROSS

1 Breakfast bread
6 ___-kiri
10 Rubik's Cube and troll dolls, once
14 Baghdad resident
15 Designer Saint Laurent
16 One-named rapper-turned-actor
17 Flu cause
18 Frisbee, checker or tiddlywink
19 Kelly of "Live! With Kelly and Michael"
20 Curved molding
21 Plains animal that tunnels
23 Region
25 Condensed books
26 Fast-food rival of Wendy's
30 Acapulco gold
31 Fit for duty, draftwise
32 Writer Jong and others
36 Voting group
38 Madrid Mrs.
40 Wild's opposite
41 "See ya!"
44 Ones under sgts., in the Army
47 Fan setting of 1, say
48 Vehicular antitheft devices
51 More nutty
54 Old geezer
55 Purchase from Google
57 Swelled heads
61 Deuce topper, in cards
62 Dumbstruck
63 New York's Memorial ___-Kettering hospital
64 Brontë's "Jane ___"
65 "First, ___ harm"
66 Warm 59-Down greeting
67 Senate majority leader Harry
68 Conclusions
69 Easy-to-catch hit . . . or what 1-, 21-, 26-, 48- and 55-Across all do

DOWN

1 Record for later viewing, in a way
2 Not a copy: Abbr.
3 Swiss river
4 Mouse's sound
5 "___ the season to be jolly"
6 Infuses with water
7 Adidas alternative
8 Dwell
9 Give credit (to)
10 Way out in an emergency
11 Tums targets
12 Train station
13 Does' mates
21 Ivy League school in Philly
22 Stravinsky or Sikorsky
24 ___ de Janeiro
26 Steve of Apple
27 "Alice's Restaurant" singer Guthrie
28 Snazzy
29 Brother of Chico and Groucho
33 Class after trig
34 Run ___ (go wild)
35 Puts in stitches
37 Nutty
39 Guacamole ingredients
42 Depilatory brand
43 Lobbed weapon
45 Trampled (on)
46 ___-mo (instant replay feature)
49 Tapped, as experience
50 Verdi opera
51 Bad-check passer
52 How a ham sandwich may be prepared
53 Former "S.N.L." comic Cheri
56 Take care of, as a garden
58 Sticky stuff
59 Obama's birthplace
60 Jacket fastener
63 Tree juice

by Johanna Fenimore and Andrea Carla Michaels

18 EASY

ACROSS

1 Self-descriptive crossword answer
5 Collar stiffener
11 Proof ender
14 Evening, in Italy
15 Port ENE of Cleveland, O.
16 Water, to Watteau
17 Spring warming
18 *Beverly Hills shopping district
20 *Lead singer of the Kinks
22 Hotfoots it
23 Reduced-price
24 ___ May of "The Beverly Hillbillies"
27 Words sung "with love" in a 1967 #1 hit?
30 Withdrawal charge
34 Musical key appropriate for an apartment dweller?
37 *It might stretch a seventh-inning stretch
39 What it takes to tango
40 Corporate division, informally . . . or a hint to the answers to the eight starred clues
41 "To ___ is human . . ."
42 *Hora, e.g.
45 Raisin, originally
47 "Shucks, you're too kind!"
48 ___ Selassie
50 Traffic stopper?
52 Like many a Mr. Bean skit
56 Tea variety
59 *"James and the Giant Peach" author
62 *Fertile area where a stream empties into an ocean
65 Gun belt contents
66 What an ET pilots
67 TV addict, slangily
68 Cry
69 Fruity red wine, familiarly
70 Nap
71 Shows signs of wanting to nap

DOWN

1 "The Jetsons" dog
2 "Borstal Boy" author Brendan
3 Donkey sounds
4 *Numbers fed into a computer
5 Starts a rally
6 "Star Trek: T.N.G." counselor
7 Helper
8 Witherspoon of "Legally Blonde"
9 Sharkey's rank, in '70s TV
10 "You ___ me at 'hello'"
11 Long-reigning English monarch, informally
12 Roof overhang
13 Requirement for union membership
19 Wynken or Blynken, e.g., but not Nod
21 Very much
25 Alight
26 Inc. relative
28 Ayatollah's home
29 One-story home
31 Subject of a Spot check?
32 Lawman Wyatt
33 Literary Jane
34 Gillette brand
35 "Take that as you will," in Internet shorthand
36 Extended
38 The thought that counts?
40 Motorola cellphone
43 "Your wish is my command" speaker
44 Org. for 50-Acrosses
45 Pleased
46 *1984 Patrick Swayze film set in the cold war
49 Repeated cry from the White Rabbit
51 Statement of faith
53 Small screen appearance
54 "Arabian Nights" prince
55 Sits (down)
56 Texas senator Ted
57 Old platter player
58 "___ calling!"
60 A little of this, a little of that
61 Completely
63 Campground parkers, for short
64 Racket

by Tim Croce

ACROSS

1 In ___ (existing)
5 Amorphous mass
9 One of the Three B's of classical music
13 Fox series set in William McKinley High School
14 Tibia or fibula
15 Singer Abdul
16 Original maker of a 38-Across
18 Moving about
19 Huge hit
20 Light horse-drawn carriage with one seat
22 Boxer who floated like a butterfly, stung like a bee
25 Japanese sash
26 Ingredients in a 38-Across
34 Weight-loss program
35 Amigo
36 Ranee's wrap
37 ___ of Capri
38 Sweet treat
41 Deadly poison
42 Mascara problem
44 Dress (up)
45 Lone Star State sch. near the Rio Grande
46 Ingredient in a 38-Across
50 Steve Martin's "King ___"
51 Hullabaloo
52 Joke you've heard many times before
57 Fragrant wood
62 Acoustic
63 Ingredient in a 38-Across
66 Haggard with 38 #1 country hits
67 Sea creature with pincers
68 Boutique
69 "Hey . . . over here!"
70 Sharer's word
71 Classic trees on shady streets

DOWN

1 They're bought by the dozen
2 Thin
3 Song word repeated after "Que"
4 Fish caught in pots
5 Original "Monty Python" airer
6 Brit's toilet
7 Burden
8 Gambler
9 Big party
10 Volvo or VW
11 Video segment
12 Tortoise racer
15 Freaks out in fear
17 Bygone head of Iran
21 Attorney's org.
23 200 in the Indianapolis 500
24 Muslim leader
26 Gadget
27 Found a new tenant for
28 Mr. T's TV group
29 Draper's material
30 Afghani capital
31 Muse of poetry
32 Extend, as a lease
33 Ooze
34 Gossip, slangily
39 Capital of Italia
40 "Heavens to Betsy!"
43 Worrisome engine noise
47 Try for a political office
48 Building material applied with a trowel
49 Bananas
52 Place to eat a 38-Across
53 Tints
54 Blunders
55 NaCl
56 Drive-___
58 ". . . or ___!"
59 Author Roald
60 Isotope, e.g.
61 Sales force, informally
64 Blade in a boat
65 David Letterman's network

by Robert Seminara

20 EASY

ACROSS

1 Lose one's amateur status
6 Prohibit
9 Mountain top?
15 Suss out
16 What may be under a mountaintop
17 Boehner's predecessor as House speaker
18 Being an online creep, in a way
21 Tupperware piece
22 Garage occupier
23 Like the rarer blood types, typically: Abbr.
24 Oscars category
30 Port of Spain
31 Test taken by a sr.
32 Ratchet (up)
33 Black cat running across one's path, say
34 Psychedelic experience
35 Violinist Perlman
38 Son of, in Arabic names
39 Tito Puente specialty
41 Many a football play
42 Proceed quietly
44 Lover of Psyche
45 Shakespearean manipulator
46 ___ avis
47 Intl. commerce group
48 Miniature map, maybe
49 Square root of -1, e.g.
53 Parisian pronoun
54 Asian title of respect
55 It's south of Eur.
56 Popular app . . . or a hint to the starts of 18-, 24- and 49-Across
64 Melodic
65 It's found near a temple
66 Gets close to
67 Folk singer Pete
68 Density symbol, in physics
69 Trimming tool

DOWN

1 Internet picture file
2 "Leaving ___ Jet Plane"
3 Army one-striper: Abbr.
4 Lands, as a fish
5 Expedia rival
6 "Bad call, ref!"
7 Ship that was double-booked?
8 Lifesavers, of a sort
9 Messy barbecue dish
10 Kenan's Nickelodeon pal
11 Sort
12 Be inventive with language
13 Ed of "Up"
14 Word with bank or back
19 "Hmm, that's unexpected"
20 Scotsman's cap
24 Disney deer
25 Minnesota city SW of Minneapolis so named for its fertile soil
26 The giant in "Jack and the Beanstalk," e.g.
27 Person whose books make a killing?
28 Grp. with peacekeeping forces
29 Celebrity gossip website
30 San Francisco's ___ Tower
34 Nickname of basketball's Allen Iverson
36 Boring tool
37 Muscle problem
39 "A Sorta Fairytale" singer Amos
40 Apollo 11 goal
43 Kids' game
45 Keep it in the family?
48 "Don't worry about me"
49 Opening words of "A Tale of Two Cities"
50 Alan who wrote "V for Vendetta"
51 Man's name that sounds like two letters of the alphabet
52 Old Mideast grp.
57 Labrador, e.g.
58 St. Paul-to-St. Louis dir.
59 "Told you so!"
60 Slangy hairdo
61 Constant faultfinder
62 Rap's Dr. ___
63 Belarus, once: Abbr.

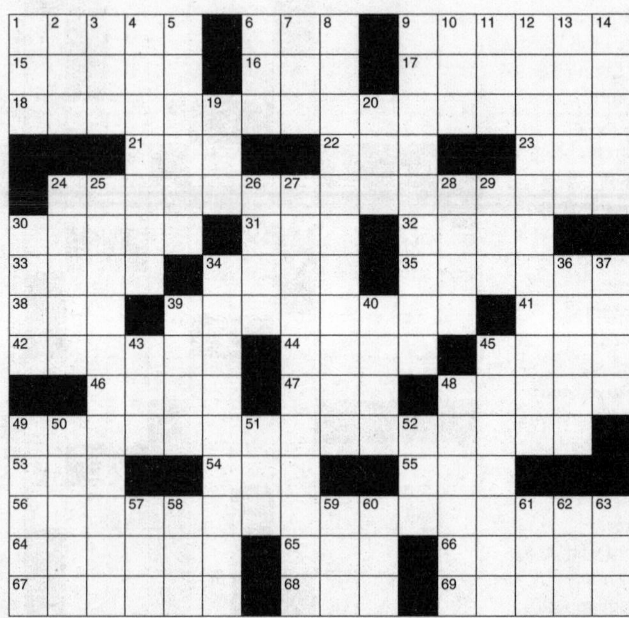

by Joel Fagliano

ACROSS

1 Tennessee team, for short
5 Acknowledge as true
10 Pole or Czech
14 Admit openly
15 Often-maligned relative
16 ___ mind
17 Blue-skinned race in "Avatar"
18 With 50-Across, it's represented by 15 squares in an appropriate arrangement in this puzzle
19 Some Monopoly purchases: Abbr.
20 French pupil
22 Grandpa on "The Simpsons"
23 Boot
24 Live it up
26 N.F.L. player with a black helmet
28 Hebrew month when Hanukkah starts
30 Richard Branson's airline company
33 Hundred Acre Wood resident
34 Place to hear fire and brimstone
38 Personal question?
39 Washing machine contents
41 David of "The Pink Panther"
42 Rear half of a griffin
43 Writer Katherine ___ Porter
44 Barely adequate
45 Iams competitor
46 1943 penny material
48 Suffix with meth- or prop-
49 What you might buy a flight with
50 See 18-Across
53 Place with complimentary bathrobes
56 Pronoun for Miss Piggy
57 Rodeway ___
58 Past the expiration date
61 Ship sinker
63 Pep up
65 "Not my call"
66 Words of encouragement
67 Calls it quits
68 Weatherproofing stuff

DOWN

1 Revolver with the letters N-E-W-S
2 Speed skater's path
3 Make-out session spot
4 Spin, as an office chair
5 It might be bummed
6 Basketball player who starred in "Kazaam"
7 Commoner
8 Police stun gun
9 "I ___ you one"
10 Barber, at times
11 Medical directive
12 With, on le menu
13 Item under a jacket, maybe
21 At any time
23 Nefarious
25 Roulette bet
27 ___-garde
28 Caffeine-laden nuts
29 "Not gonna happen"
31 Comment made while crossing one's fingers
32 Pitchers' hitless games, in baseball slang
35 Experienced through another
36 The first Mrs. Trump
37 Shakespeare's Antonio and Bassanio, e.g.
40 Judge
42 Reclined
47 British sailors
49 One of the friends on "Friends"
51 No-show in a Beckett play
52 Certain belly button
53 Tuxedo shirt button
54 St. Peter was the first
55 B.A. part
58 Cabo's peninsula
59 Lots
60 Thing often of interest?
62 Hawaiian dish
64 Blanc or Brooks

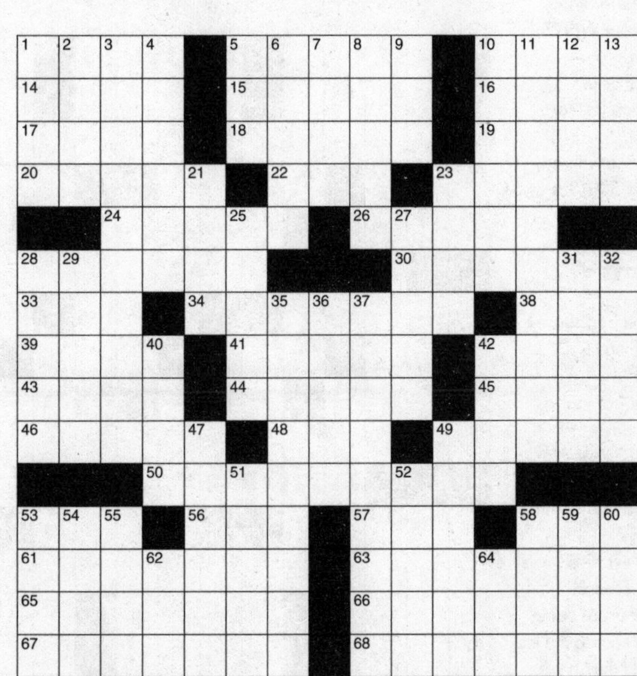

by Joel Fagliano

22 EASY

ACROSS

1 Pat down, as pipe tobacco
5 Trade
9 Carpenter's file
13 Grammy winner McLachlan
14 Heading on a list of errands
15 Salt lake state
16 1959 hit by the Drifters
19 Stock market index, with "the"
20 Collaborative Web project
21 Helpers
22 What children should be, and not heard, they say
24 Pudding or pie
27 1970 hit by Eric Clapton
32 Barbie and others
34 180° from WNW
35 Close by
36 Letter after pi
37 Belly muscles, for short
40 Magazine with an annual "500" list
42 ___-la-la
43 Forever and ever
45 "___ in apple"
47 Nutso
49 1978 hit by Journey
53 Something to scribble on
54 "Hurry!," on an order
57 11- or 12-year-old
60 Therefore
62 One may be under a blouse
63 What the artists of 16-, 27- and 49-Across are doing (in reference to the last words of their hits)?
67 "___ and the King of Siam"
68 On the Adriatic, say
69 Brings in, as a salary
70 Piece of fly-casting equipment
71 Roseanne, before and after Arnold
72 Exercise that may involve sitting cross-legged

DOWN

1 California/Nevada border lake
2 "Can anybody hear us?"
3 Feb. follower
4 "Close call!"
5 Bram who created Dracula
6 "Alas!"
7 Billboards, e.g.
8 Certain lap dog, informally
9 Gloat
10 Slightly
11 Kemo ___ (the Lone Ranger)
12 ___ ed. (gym class)
13 Norms: Abbr.
17 Nobel-winning author André
18 Fisherman's tale
23 Org. for the Bears and Bengals
25 "But of course, amigo!"
26 Garden of ___
28 Fed. air marshal's org.
29 Locale for an 1863 address
30 "B.C." creator Johnny
31 A waiter carries plates on it
32 Sketched
33 Cry before "I know!"
38 Worms, to a fisherman
39 Not at all nutso
41 Network with an "eye" for entertainment
44 Dakar's land
46 Pearly Gates sentinel
48 Alias letters
50 Anderson of "WKRP in Cincinnati"
51 "That's so funny I forgot to laugh"
52 Rim
55 ___ football
56 Fail's opposite
57 Bygone Kremlin resident
58 Cabernet, for one
59 Feminine suffix
61 Follow, as orders
64 Arrest
65 Fed. property manager
66 Philosopher ___-tzu

by Amy Johnson

ACROSS

1 With 1-Across, toy train
5 Set of values
10 Half of cuatro
13 ___ mark (#)
14 Texas city
15 Messenger ___
16 Introductory drawing class
17 Old game consoles
18 Early Tarzan Ron
19 Not found
21 With 21-Across, "I'll believe it when I see it!"
23 With 23-Across, CBer's opening
26 With 26-Across, #1 hit for the Mamas & the Papas
27 ___ Doone (cookie brand)
28 Prefix with center
31 Jobs at Apple
32 Six-pointers, in brief
33 Med. exam involving an injection into the forearm
36 "Washingtons"
37 With 37-Across and 37-Across, a holiday song
39 Lead-in to girl
42 Tots
43 ___ Records
46 Play lazily, as a guitar
48 Rap's Dr. ___
49 Thai or Taiwanese
51 With 51-Across, town crier's cry
53 With 53-Across, "Nothing's changed"
55 With 55-Across and 55-Across, real-estate catchphrase
58 Real nerve
59 ___ Records
60 Montana's capital
62 "The lady ___ protest too much"
65 "Perfect" number
66 Part of a train headed to a refinery
67 Drama award since 1956
68 The "E" in E.S.L.: Abbr.
69 Drenches
70 With 70-Across, #1 hit for Billy Idol

DOWN

1 With 1-Down and 1-Down, lively Latin dance
2 With 2-Down, "Ver-r-ry funny!"
3 Stable employees
4 Buckeye
5 Sup
6 "Shut yer ___!"
7 Title for Goethe
8 "Green thumb" or "purple prose"
9 Universe
10 German city rebuilt after W.W. II
11 Temporarily away
12 Agrees
14 With 14-Down, like some talk shows
20 Play in the N.H.L.
22 Being pulled
23 Diner inits.
24 Curtain holder
25 Made tighter, as a knot
29 With 29-Down, nursery rhyme starter
30 Debatables
34 "As an aside," in chat lingo
35 Big inits. in C&W
37 First lady before Michelle
38 ___ bin Laden
39 Jock
40 1976 horror film whose remake was released, appropriately, on 6/6/06
41 Copying exactly, as a sketch
43 1970 John Wayne western
44 Baseball's Ripken
45 &
47 Collection of legends
50 Hardly ever
52 Farm letters?
54 With 54-Down, food gelling agent
56 Spanish pot
57 Bottle part
61 "Illmatic" rapper
63 With 63-Down, title boy in a 2011 Spielberg film
64 With 64-Down and 64-Down, Fat Albert's catchphrase

by Tim Croce

24 EASY

ACROSS

1 Scotch ___
5 Stare dumbfoundedly
9 Simba's best friend in "The Lion King"
13 Nyet : Russian :: ___ : German
14 More than some
15 Engine
16 Jamaican sprinter nicknamed "The Fastest Man on Earth"
18 Story for storage
19 Polynesian kingdom
20 Nothing daring in terms of offerings
22 Ostentatious displays
24 Sounded like a horn
25 Washtub
27 Indian dress
28 Mediterranean and Caribbean
30 Winter pear
32 Having painterish pretensions
36 Golf course target
37 PC outlet
39 Had supper
40 Firebug's crime
42 Lovett of country music
43 Title beekeeper in a 1997 film
44 "Dies ___" (hymn)
46 Brand of dinnerware with a Scandinavian design
48 Bandleader Glenn
51 Roger who played 007
53 Service charges
57 Apple tablets
59 "Dig?"
60 Heralded, as a new era
62 Rum drinks for British sailors
63 Subway support
64 Companion of the Pinta and Santa Maria
65 Cravings
66 Pig's grunt
67 "General Hospital," e.g.

DOWN

1 Letter-shaped fastener
2 Fable writer
3 Nightspots for cocktails and easy listening
4 Mysteries
5 Yak
6 Baseball's Matty or Jesus
7 D.C. types
8 "___, Brute?"
9 Sore loser's cry
10 Fragrance of roses
11 France's longest river
12 Shaped like a rainbow
15 Teen hanging out among shoppers
17 Dozes
21 "The ___ Daba Honeymoon"
23 Brothers and sisters, for short
26 Aristocratic
27 Bawl out
28 Place that might offer mud baths
29 Pointy part of Mr. Spock
31 007, for one
33 Rush Limbaugh medium
34 Sault ___ Marie, Mich.
35 "___-haw!"
37 Turmoils
38 500 sheets
41 Structures in the Gulf of Mexico
43 Annual tournaments . . . or a description of the starts of 16-, 20-, 37-, 53- and 60-Across?
45 Terrier's sound
47 Roulette bet that's not rouge
48 Hot and humid
49 River of Grenoble, France
50 Divulge
52 Minneapolis suburb
54 It replaced the franc and mark
55 Actor Morales
56 Body part that's often bumped
58 Partner of Crackle and Pop
61 "Benevolent" club member

by Zhouqin Burnikel and D. Scott Nichols

ACROSS

1 Cowboy chow
5 Distresses
9 Word from the Arabic for "struggle"
14 Simpson who said "Beneath my goody two shoes lie some very dark socks"
15 See 16-Across
16 With 15-Across, preparing to pop the question, say
17 Cash dispensers, for short
18 "___ first you don't succeed . . ."
19 What a star on a U.S. flag represents
20 Subject of the book "Revolution in the Valley"
22 Beset by a curse
23 Pinocchio, periodically
24 Snarling dog
25 Poisonous
28 Person who works with dipsticks
33 Not much, in cookery
34 Powerful org. with HQ in Fairfax, Va.
35 Shine, commercially
37 People in this may have big ears
42 Shot ___
43 "Criminy!"
44 Actress Watts
45 Sioux shoe
49 Metaphor, e.g.
50 "Whazzat?"
51 Employs
53 Meal with Elijah's cup
56 Journalist of the Progressive Era
61 Kick out
62 Vogue alternative
63 Starting score in tennis
64 Techie sorts
65 From the top
66 Managed, with "out"
67 Unable to hold still
68 Speaker's place
69 Like Lindbergh's historic trans-Atlantic flight

DOWN

1 Glitz
2 Meter maid of song
3 Gomer Pyle's org.
4 Legendary lizard with a fatal gaze
5 Japanese dog breed
6 Notify
7 Pastures
8 Brother of Cain and Abel
9 Book after Deuteronomy
10 Person getting on-the-job training
11 Snopes.com subject
12 Upfront stake
13 Monopoly card
21 Specialty
24 Cartoonist Addams
25 Pack down
26 Detestation
27 ___ knife
29 Japanese mushroom
30 Grand ___ (wine of the highest rank)
31 Eskimo home
32 Stick together
36 Theater award since 1956
38 Word repeatedly sung after "She loves you . . ."
39 "___ amis"
40 Opposite of exit
41 Deals at a dealership
46 Partner of balances
47 Girl's show of respect
48 Cell centers
52 Twists, as facts
53 Gaming giant
54 Smooth
55 Lighten up?
56 Quaff for Beowulf
57 Bone next to the radius
58 Gorilla pioneering in sign language
59 Knievel of motorcycle stunts
60 Make over

by Patrick Blindauer and Andrea Carla Michaels

26 MEDIUM

ACROSS

1 What quoth the raven?
4 Moving well for one's age
8 1988 Salt-N-Pepa hit
14 Washington in D.C., e.g.
15 Idiot
16 Country on el Mediterráneo
17 Coastal inlet
18 Part of a Halloween dinner?
20 Girl in tartan
22 Moisten, in a way
23 Upstate N.Y. college
24 Soft-shell clam
27 "Prince Igor" composer
29 Part of a Halloween dinner?
31 "Me neither"
32 Ways to go: Abbr.
33 Breathtaking creatures?
34 Checks out
35 Part of a Halloween dinner?
38 Pricey violin
41 Icicle site
42 ___ salad
45 Bed size
46 Part of a Halloween dinner?
49 One pushing the envelope?
51 Something found on a chemist's table
52 Certain Halloween costumes, for short
53 "Battling Bella" of '70s politics
55 State
56 Part of a Halloween dinner?
60 Man's name that's another man's name backward
61 Recruit
62 Stagehand
63 Part of the alloy britannium
64 ___ Peanut Butter Cups
65 What a colon represents in an emoticon
66 Heart chart: Abbr.

DOWN

1 Fast-food chain with a smiling star in its logo
2 Flew
3 Deceitful sorts
4 Part of GPS: Abbr.
5 Punch line?
6 Deli loaf
7 Jedi Council leader
8 Basil-based sauces
9 Walk down the aisle
10 Lotion inits.
11 Bob and others
12 Give rise to
13 Pastes used in Middle Eastern cuisine
19 Publisher's ID
21 Pizzeria owner in "Do the Right Thing"
25 "Whoops"
26 Jet
28 ___ impulse
30 Heretofore
34 Thick, sweet liqueur
35 Tilt
36 "Jeopardy!" column
37 Cameo shape
38 First pope
39 Black and blue, say
40 Savory deep-fried pastry
42 Lift
43 Not brand-name
44 Spare wear
46 Nuns' wear
47 Dix + 1
48 Org. with a snake in its logo
50 Billiards trick shot
54 Impulse
57 "___ So Sweet to Trust in Jesus"
58 Say "I do" when you don't?
59 Groovy music?

by Joel Fagliano

MEDIUM 27

ACROSS

1 Universal Studios role of 1941
8 1-Across, in 23-Down
15 Not yet delivered
16 Thank you, in Tokyo
17 Universal Studios role of 1931
18 17-Across, in 23-Down
19 Gas grade
20 D.C. baseballer
21 Young socialite
22 Rapscallion
23 Clusterfist
25 Carnivorous fish
28 Through
29 "I beg to differ"
33 Shetland Islands sight
34 Unsettle
35 "St. Matthew Passion" composer, for short
36 Bit of chicken feed
37 What some hotel balconies overlook
39 Low reef
40 Like patent leather
43 Moon, e.g., to a poet
44 A, in Austria
45 Genesis wife
46 Genesis craft
47 Green touches?
48 Calls
50 Show age, in a way
51 U. of Miami's athletic org.
54 "Aladdin" monkey
55 Some bait
59 Universal Studios role of 1925
61 59-Across, in 23-Down
62 Starts gently
63 Comic strip infant
64 Universal Studios role of 1931
65 64-Across, in 23-Down

DOWN

1 Namby-pamby
2 ___ about (approximately)
3 Crescent shape
4 Second-largest city in Ark.
5 Period of focusing on oneself
6 "Your 15 minutes of fame ___!"
7 An I.Q. of about 100, e.g.
8 C. S. Lewis setting
9 Fields
10 Nickname for a 2012 presidential candidate
11 Ends of some close N.F.L. games: Abbr.
12 Secure, as a contract
13 Plains native
14 Development site
23 Things worth looking into?
24 Hold up
25 Trudges (through)
26 Furry folivore
27 Phoenix or Washington
28 Brewery fixture
30 Implied
31 Meager
32 "That's for sure!"
34 Crested bird
35 One-two part
38 Peeve
41 Glum
42 Acupressure technique
44 Pacific Northwest city
46 Barnard grad, e.g.
47 Stickum
49 Intensely stirred up
50 Winter forecast
51 Made like
52 Scorch
53 La mía es la tuya, they say
55 Some online communications, briefly
56 Part of graduation attire
57 Start of 19 John Grisham novel titles
58 Place to be pampered
60 Asian electronics giant

by David Kwong

28 MEDIUM

ACROSS

1 Bust targets
6 Rumple
10 Group that inspired "Mamma Mia!"
14 Time for vampires
15 [gasp!]
16 Johnny Unitas, for most of his career
17 Can't take
18 "Don't put words in my mouth!"
20 Requests a dog treat, maybe
22 Hustler's card game
23 "I wasn't born yesterday!"
26 Special Forces wear
27 Gives a stemwinder
28 Part of "snafu"
29 "Sesame Street" viewer
30 Soup with sushi
31 Fleet
34 "Let this be our little secret" . . . with a hint to 18-, 23-, 50- or 54-Across
40 Edict locale of 1598
41 Contract period, often
42 Monopoly token
45 A.P.O. addressees
46 1966 answer to the Mustang
48 Warren Report name
50 "Wanna start somethin'?"
52 Swallower of Pinocchio
53 Take up residence
54 "Ooh, I'm shaking in my boots!"
56 Lead-in to fan or jet
60 Best Picture of 2012
61 Go a few rounds
62 Gaming pioneer
63 Big name in 59-Down exploration
64 Like a spent briquette
65 George of "Just Shoot Me!"

DOWN

1 Kind of fingerprinting
2 Slab unit, on a menu
3 "Ewww, gross!"
4 Tumbleweed locale, stereotypically
5 Bitter conflict
6 Rapid, in music
7 Relo rental, perhaps
8 Salon sound
9 Landscaper's purchase
10 John Wilkes Booth, e.g.
11 Easter wear
12 Stewed to the gills
13 Bear witness (to)
19 Former Philippine first lady ___ Marcos
21 How-___
23 Tangle untangler
24 Indy racer Luyendyk
25 Tammany tiger creator
26 Danube's color, to a Berliner
28 "Famous" cookie man
31 Small soldiers
32 Loaf with caraway seeds, maybe
33 Very soon
35 Most holes in ones
36 Camelot lady
37 Admissions honcho
38 Five-and-ten, e.g.
39 Suffix with switch
42 Elephant rider's seat
43 How driftwood may end up
44 Banjo sounds
46 The Cavs, on scoreboards
47 Japanese police dogs
49 Some saxes
50 Ark contents
51 Animator Tex
53 Treasure-hunters' aids
55 Former pres. Tyler sided with it
57 Dirt-dishing newspaper
58 It can leave a tan line
59 Texas tea

by Jacob McDermott

ACROSS

1 They're thrown from horses
7 Fake
11 "The Silence of the Lambs" org.
14 Join the game, in a way
15 Spun
16 TV ET
17 The "you" in "you caught my eye" in a 1965 #1 hit
18 Casino sights
20 It flows in the Loire
21 Pasta name suffix
23 Boss of TV's Mork
24 Small-time thieves
27 Johannes : German :: ___ : Scottish
28 O'Hare or Newark Liberty
29 Totally awesome
31 One usually buys a round one
35 Olympian Ohno
37 Some archaeological finds
39 Author of "The Prague Cemetery"
40 "Hawaii ___"
41 Suffix with drunk
42 Schleppers' aids
44 Relative of a tank top
45 "Roots" surname
47 Slip past
48 Touchdowns: Abbr.
50 Antibloating brand
51 It can cause bloating
52 German word that's 67-Across spelled backward
54 Con game
58 Glove material
60 Fool
61 It may be topped with an angel
62 What an intersection may have
65 Excavation
67 German word that's 52-Across spelled backward
68 Parthian predecessor
69 City north of Lisbon
70 Butt
71 Setting for a fall
72 Minimum

DOWN

1 Dish with melted cheese
2 Occupy
3 Just above
4 + 6
5 Some commuter "reading"
6 Joe of "NCIS"
7 Overran
8 Tramp
9 Shylock trait
10 Sharp circle?
11 Willingly, old-style
12 Nonkosher sandwich
13 Uncertainties
19 Discouraging advice
22 Japanese flower-arranging art
25 Line at a stationery store?
26 Topps collectible
30 Cataloging things
32 Fight back
33 Whacked
34 Vogue on a dance floor
35 Shaving brand
36 Place to get a bite?
38 Certain heat conduit
43 Mishmash
46 Lit
49 Ship's route
53 Familiar phone conversation starter
55 Common spice in Indian food
56 Shades
57 Cereal killer
58 Went to and fro
59 Convergent point
62 Oscar-winning John
63 Entry
64 Fence (in)
66 Word before rain, heat and gloom

by Alan Derkazarian

30 MEDIUM

ACROSS

1 Trek ending in Mecca
5 Boat with a flat bottom
9 Word heard on 39-/41-Across
14 Et ___
15 "Well, I don't think so"
16 Metallic veins
17 Bath, e.g.
18 Jessica of "Hitchcock"
19 Hand game choice
20 Hand sanitizer brand
22 Halves of sawbucks
24 Tends to
27 Made sacred
30 Treater's declaration
34 Member of the cat family
35 Coat color
37 "Egad!"
38 Gray head?
39 & 41 Annual May 1 celebration
43 "Do Ya" grp.
44 1998 Sarah McLachlan hit
46 Appear
48 Running, poetically
50 Bikes
52 Pragmatic sorts
54 Behave perfectly
56 Charlotte ___, Virgin Islands
58 Clodhopper
62 Public spat
63 "Star Wars" sister
66 Frat house alternative
67 Debussy's "___ de Lune"
68 Look like a creep
69 Chekhovian sister of Masha and Irina
70 Performances on 39-/41-Across
71 Long ago
72 Fool (with)

DOWN

1 Plucked instrument
2 Baseball family name
3 J'adore fragrance maker
4 King replaced by William and Mary
5 Temporary residence, maybe
6 Feng shui "energy"
7 Only partner?
8 Author Tobias
9 British academic exam
10 "Wouldn't It Be ___?" ("My Fair Lady" song)
11 River to the Baltic
12 Female fowl
13 Blockhead
21 Tennis great Ivan
23 Turner autobiography
25 Something watched on télévision
26 Hoopla
27 Company with a duck in its logo
28 Poor
29 Kind of acid used in making soap
31 Beer brand owned by Pabst
32 Hatch ___ (conspire)
33 Shrieks of pain
36 Pitching professionals
40 Montaigne work
42 Bulldog's place, in brief
45 Land on the Adriatic
47 Pitching stat
49 The cinema
51 Fishers with pots
53 Shining
55 Nice ___ (prude)
56 Free speech supporter: Abbr.
57 Coarse powder
59 Subversive one
60 56-Down and others: Abbr.
61 Short winter holiday?
62 Institute, e.g.: Abbr.
64 Want ad inits.
65 Suffix with hotel

by Paula Gamache

ACROSS

1 Target of union hatred
5 Weak part of a hull
9 Dormant volcano in the Cascade Range
15 H-___
16 Low bar
17 Facing
18 Literally, "itself"
19 *2007 Best Picture nominee
21 Mental lightweights
23 Sony laptop line
24 A.L. East city, on scoreboards
25 *"Hope this works!"
27 Francis, for one
28 Tackle box stock
29 A, in Altdorf
30 Many apps
31 Language suffix
32 "It's a kick in a glass" sloganeer, once
34 Old-fashioned broadcasters
35 *Irrelevant . . . or what the answers to the five starred clues have?
38 Broadcast online in real time
41 Contact lens cleaner brand
42 Little litter sound
45 Thick-veined vegetable
46 World of Warcraft event
48 New Mexico's ___ Canyon
50 "American Pie" actress Tara
51 *"Abbey Road" track
53 Coastal hunter
54 Diplomat Annan
55 Hipster
56 *Start of many limericks
59 Part of a pedestal between the base and the cornice
60 Outfielder's cry
61 Ticked off
62 Suffix with cyclo-
63 Creed
64 Bound
65 Whaleboat features

DOWN

1 Possible target for a nail gun
2 Plentiful
3 Like monastery life
4 Look around
5 Handled
6 In the real world
7 With 39-Down, hot
8 Director Van Peebles
9 Shrek creator
10 Wandering soul
11 Hole puncher
12 Island off the Gabonese coast
13 Ticket agent?
14 Lines on a package
20 "The Dark Knight Rises" villain
22 Alternatively
26 Baked
27 Match (up)
30 Whom some novelty disguises imitate
33 "Ready, ___ . . . !"
34 "This is ___"
35 Swot : Britain :: ___ : America
36 Pennsylvania's northernmost county
37 McCarthyite paranoia
38 "Forget that!"
39 See 7-Down
40 Spoils, in a way
42 Maybelline product
43 It's crossed by a center line
44 Soup dumplings
46 Modern response to hilarity
47 In
49 Maintained, as one's principles
51 Geezers
52 Fit
54 Linked
57 "I already ___"
58 Reply of faux innocence

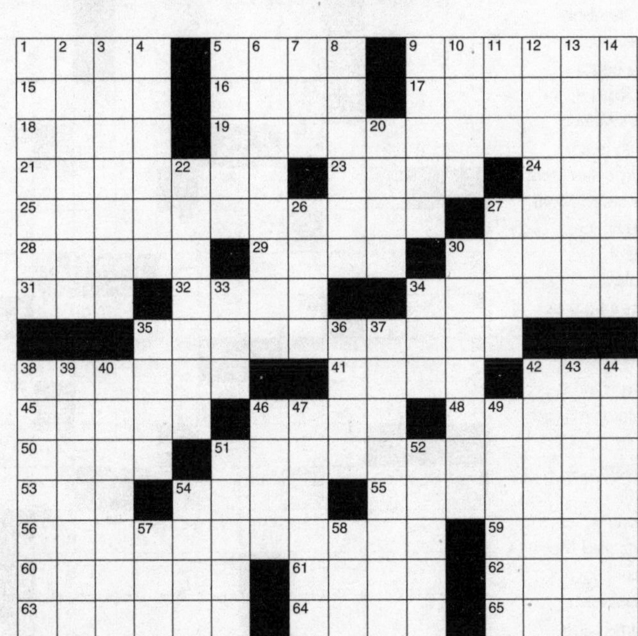

by Josh Knapp

32 MEDIUM

ACROSS

1 Not square
4 Avoid responsibilities
9 "A Passage to India" woman
14 Wall St. rating
15 TV signal part
16 Boneheads
17 N.B.A. or N.F.L. honor
18 Remembered Mom, in a way
20 Filters slowly
22 Auto financing letters
23 Greek salad staple
24 Princess, e.g.
27 Noted literary pseudonym
29 Mr. ___ (Peter Lorre film sleuth)
31 Remembered Mom, in a way
36 Zodiac symbol
38 Lamprey hunter
39 Hillbilly negative
40 Clears, as a drain
43 Hawaii's Mauna ___
44 Dim with tears
46 Typical political talk
48 Remembered Mom, in a way
51 City SE of Honolulu
52 Princess who was captured by Jabba the Hutt
53 Dashing Flynn
55 Pieces in a Mideast armory
58 Famous rescue vessel
60 ___ manual
63 Remembered Mom, in a way
67 Bankbook abbr.
68 Chocolate base
69 Employs soap and water
70 Old Mideast alliance, for short
71 Motorist's problem
72 "Cheers" role
73 Meddle

DOWN

1 Certain radio enthusiasts
2 Roof part
3 It may be on a roll
4 Having an attitude
5 "Say that again?"
6 With 25-Down, 1979 exile
7 "Hope & Faith" actress Kelly
8 Ted once of ABC News
9 Focusing problem, for short
10 G.I., in old slang
11 Falco of "Nurse Jackie"
12 Sleeping site, maybe
13 Terrier in whodunits
19 ___ Stanley Gardner
21 What "D" means
25 See 6-Down
26 Ho Chi Minh Trail locale
28 Words before a clarification
29 "The Rachel Maddow Show" carrier
30 Florida's ___ National Forest
32 Emcee's delivery
33 Extremely agitated
34 Lubricate again
35 Harry Potter villain Malfoy
37 Make a mush of
41 Words of woe
42 ___ of the realm
45 Like a blockbuster's cast, often
47 Cries of discovery
49 Lifebuoy competitor
50 Lloyd of the silents
54 Charlotte ___ (cream-filled dessert)
55 Law enforcers at sea: Abbr.
56 Enthusiasm
57 ___ Empire (bygone domain)
59 Title river in 1957's Best Picture
61 Sit on it
62 Not even close to creaky
64 Opposition
65 "Die Meistersinger" soprano
66 Cartoon Chihuahua

DIAGONAL

1 Annual message

by Bruce Venzke

ACROSS

1 Allowing some ventilation, say
5 ___ in the park
10 Org. with Divisions I, II and III
14 Teen woe
15 Singer or actor's helper
17 Interstitially, say
19 Brit's tea ___
20 Hosts prefer them
21 "___ see"
22 Nina ___ (fashion label)
26 Keep an ___ (watch)
28 Wearer of a red-starred tiara
31 Bitter herb
32 One in the doghouse?
33 Card reader, briefly
34 '40s blowups
36 Modern electric cars
40 Tokyo strip?
42 Kind of screen
46 Grant or Carter
47 Marquee actress
50 Twofold
52 Verso's flip side
53 Explanation that doesn't explain anything, informally
54 Surname in punk rock
56 Follower of a list of names
58 May delivery
63 "Why bother?!"
64 Title parent in a TLC reality series
65 Coop sound
66 Plot line
67 Northern duck

DOWN

1 Government rep.
2 Cartoon character with shades
3 Fats Domino's first name
4 Melees
5 Caesar's greeting
6 Captured
7 Island in the Thames
8 "To life!"
9 Start for a shipbuilder
10 Like melees
11 Runs along
12 Beats, as the competition
13 Sounds at a fireworks display
16 Lawyer's need
18 Literary character who says "Gentle reader, may you never feel what I then felt!"
21 Personal letters
23 Declaration that might precede a fold
24 100 lbs.
25 Can
27 Super ___
29 Children's author who won three Edgars
30 Bless, in a way
35 Title boy in a 1964 Disney film
36 Space maker
37 Certain monarchy
38 Nerve junction
39 Solder and others
41 Certain lighter or highlighter
43 Driving surface
44 Flatter servilely
45 End of a school series
48 Dark circle
49 Attendee
51 Boost, as sound
55 The Rio Grande divides it: Abbr.
57 Clucks of disappointment
58 In
59 Neighbor of 55-Down
60 Confucian scholar Chu ___
61 End of a count?
62 Poison source in Christie's "A Pocket Full of Rye"

by Patrick Merrell

34 MEDIUM

ACROSS

1 1983 Tony-winning musical
5 In-crowd invitees
10 Soap brand that contains pumice
14 One on a one-dollar bill
15 Pool hall equipment
16 Site of the first human sin
17 Good stretch for the Dow
19 Microsoft Word menu pick
20 Mottled bean
21 "No lie!"
23 Extra after a movie's credits, perhaps
27 Try to impress at a party, say
30 "Every kiss begins . . ." jeweler
31 State firmly
32 Fritz's "Forget it!"
34 Annoying
38 Oxy 5 target
39 2006 Jay-Z single
41 ___ Cruces, N.M.
42 Its license plates have the motto "Famous Potatoes"
44 Dog that bit Miss Gulch
45 Lose oomph
46 Pitcher Dennis in Cooperstown, for short
48 Reflect deeply on
50 Midas service
53 Ingenue's quality
54 Chris Matthews's channel
58 Conical woodwind
59 Cry accompanying the arrival of visitors
63 Target of a narc
64 Hawaiian veranda
65 Home of Qom
66 Gas brand in Canada
67 Download on a Nook
68 ___ Neuf (Parisian landmark)

DOWN

1 Zodiacal border
2 Prefix with lock or skid
3 When tripled, 1965 Byrds hit
4 Suffocate
5 Falklands War side: Abbr.
6 Postgraduate field
7 Beverage store bagful
8 Length of yarn
9 "Shame on you!"
10 A bionic part of Steve Austin
11 Deck out
12 Concert hall, e.g.
13 "I'm in" indicator
18 Reason to deny bar service
22 Suffix with land or mind
24 Bond villain
25 Biblical verb
26 Prime example
27 W.W. II foe
28 Ardent
29 Self-referential, informally
33 Still in bed
35 Czech, for one
36 Film character based on Hearst
37 North Sea feeder
39 John who wrote "What worries you, masters you"
40 The Big Easy
43 Forcible dismissal
45 Church activity
47 ___ corn (sweet-and-salty snack)
49 Gimlet garnish
50 Toyland characters
51 Civil eruptions
52 Addict's need, informally
53 Iditarod terminus
55 Emperor after Claudius
56 Fiber source
57 Small change in the eurozone
60 Brian who composed the "Microsoft sound"
61 Former hoopster ___ Ming
62 English comedian Mayall

by David Sullivan

ACROSS

1 Wine's partner
5 Overflow
9 Y's
14 Spingarn of the N.A.A.C.P.'s Spingarn Medal
15 Astronomical effect
16 Broadway musical that opens with "Maybe"
17 List shortener
18 Come again?
19 Mammal that hums to its young
20 Language that gave us "kowtow"
23 "I know that one!"
24 Rough shelter
28 Clutch performer?
34 Kaplan course subj.
35 "Right You Are, Mr. ___" (1957 novel)
36 "___ aren't the droids you're looking for" ("Star Wars" line)
37 On
38 God-fearing
40 The Wildcats of the N.C.A.A.
41 Like some photos
44 Winter playground
45 Hardly Mr. Personality
46 Discuss reasonable outcomes upfront
49 Generic
50 Gent, in Britain
51 Emergency shout . . . or a possible title for this puzzle
58 One providing assistance after a crash
61 Nonentity
62 Hayseed
63 Filling in a gordita
64 Help list, e.g.
65 It's got all the answers
66 Cosmetician's goof
67 Per
68 ___ Anglia

DOWN

1 Entertained at a reception, maybe
2 Ninth in a series
3 Almost
4 Canadian P.M. Pierre Trudeau's middle name
5 1931 film for which Wallace Beery won Best Actor
6 Piece by piece
7 All the way through 12th grade, informally
8 It goes through many phases
9 Least genuine
10 Restrained, as a dog
11 Biology subject
12 One of the Kardashians
13 Setting for much of Homer's "Odyssey"
21 Scand. land
22 Skull and Bones member
25 Baseball Hall-of-Famer nicknamed Knucksie
26 Give, as a little extra
27 Tops
28 Funny Tracey
29 Often-grated cheese
30 Thin sheet metal
31 Bête ___
32 Unresponsive?
33 Put up, in a way
39 The English Beat, for one
42 Red, white and blue players
43 Clint Eastwood, for one
45 Split
47 Hotel room amenity
48 Where Archimedes had his "Eureka!" moment
52 L. Frank Baum princess
53 No. 2
54 ___ Rapee, longtime Radio City Music Hall conductor
55 Mysterious glow
56 Babe Ruth's 2,220, for short
57 2012 campaign issue
58 Thinking figs.
59 Rum ___ Tugger ("Cats" cat)
60 "You don't say!"

by Brendan Emmett Quigley and Elizabeth Donovan

36 MEDIUM

ACROSS

1 Afro-Cuban dance
6 Chief exec
10 Strained-at bug, in an idiom
14 Crazy as ___
15 Credits listing
16 Get in a lather
17 Complaints about a Kentucky fort?
19 Hatchet man
20 Hearing range
21 No-goodnik
23 "Winter's Bone" heroine ___ Dolly
24 Hebrew letter before nun
26 Soon, to a bard
27 Cohort of Athos
30 Party desirables
33 Moved like a dragonfly
36 Place a levy on pushpins?
38 Digger's strike
39 Cause to topple
41 Mauna ___
42 Security for smoked salmon?
44 Paul of "Mad About You"
46 "Specifically . . ."
47 Hasbro action figures
49 Severely reprimand, with "out"
51 Kevin Bacon degree count
52 "Take Me Bak ___" (1972 Slade song)
55 Polar bear's resting spot
58 Bottom-line red ink
61 Mid 13th-century year
62 Piles of old soul records?
64 "My Way" lyricist
65 Eyelid malady
66 Catchall category
67 Classic computer game, or its island world
68 Gain from a quarterback sneak, perhaps
69 Nectar-yielding fruits

DOWN

1 Do some fall cleanup
2 ___ nerve (funny bone part)
3 "Sicko" documentarian
4 Prime spot at a theater
5 Hippie's cross
6 For the time being
7 "Arabian Nights" menace
8 "Benevolent" order
9 Keebler cracker brand
10 Breakfast bar stuff
11 Say no to some pro basketballers?
12 On the calm side
13 Okla., until 1907
18 Given to wanderlust
22 Where "K-I-S-S-I-N-G" occurs, as taunting kids say
25 Cell division
28 Double-check the addition of
29 Discount, in store names
31 ___-Ball (arcade game)
32 Despot until 1917
33 Dimwit
34 Suffix with buck
35 Critic Reed does major damage?
37 Reproduces, in a way
40 U.P.S. delivery: Abbr.
43 Not be rumpled, say
45 Put in solitary
48 Born under a bad sign
50 Like the north sides of some trees
53 Starbucks order
54 Glacial ridge
55 Mosque leader
56 Big Apple sch.
57 ___ James, singer played by Beyoncé
59 'Vette roof option
60 Ukr. and Lith., once
63 Firth of Clyde port

by Kevin Christian

ACROSS

1 "Twilight" author Stephenie
6 Green of TV's "Robot Chicken"
10 Texas' ___ Ranch
13 "The Faerie Queene" woman
14 Like typical law school programs
16 Store with a red star logo
17 Some Monopoly purchases
18 With 50-Across, how one can tell that this puzzle was up all night waiting to be solved?
20 Mattress problem
21 Churchill, e.g.
25 Setting of Camus's "The Stranger"
29 Mike holders
32 Not merely a
33 Genteel affairs
34 Firebrand
36 "I haven't made up my mind"
40 Hysterical states
41 Language whose alphabet reads from right to left
42 Some of Vanna's letters?
43 Hosp. staffers
44 Suggests
47 Old Testament book: Abbr.
49 Crumbly topping
50 See 18-Across
58 Nobelists, e.g.
61 Spooky sound
62 Tennis players in action
63 ___ Blaine, protagonist of F. Scott Fitzgerald's "This Side of Paradise"
64 ___ de Montréal
65 A shot in the arm, say
66 Grammy winner Lou

DOWN

1 Actress Rogers
2 "In principio ___ Verbum" (biblical phrase)
3 "Bleah!"
4 2006 Grammy winner for "Amarantine"
5 Scrap
6 Quick
7 Representative Cantor
8 Bluffer's giveaway
9 "Take it!"
10 Bucolic setting
11 Fraudulent, say
12 Third class?: Abbr.
14 Some salon jobs
15 Baseball manager Ned
19 Snarler, of a sort
22 Whiskered beasts
23 Fleming of "Spellbound"
24 Ump's cry
25 Side effect of a withdrawal?
26 Catches wind of
27 Most festive
28 Info on the reverse of a title page: Abbr.
29 "High Society" studio
30 The sculpture "Kryptos" sits outside its hdqrs.
31 Pen
34 Idiot
35 Border
37 Old Testament book: Abbr.
38 Female half
39 Some M.I.T. grads
44 Five-time world figure skating champion Carol
45 Big corp. in the aerospace industry
46 Org. whose members wear fire-resistant clothing
48 Cast
49 Part of la famille
51 Call for
52 "Me say" this word in a 1957 hit
53 Hot times in Haiti
54 Columnist Bombeck
55 "Yikes!"
56 ___ of Warwick (War of the Roses figure)
57 "The ___ the limit"
58 Mid first-century year
59 Company with a "Running Man" symbol
60 Diminutive suffix

by David Levinson Wilk

38 MEDIUM

ACROSS

1 "___ dat?"
4 Twain adventurer
10 Calorific
14 With "in" and 2-Down, with respectful humility
15 Spicy cuisine
16 Biblical progenitor of the Edomites
17 Producer of seven U2 albums
18 "Messiah" composer
19 With "in" and 12-Down, as a precaution
20 Son of Henry Ford
22 Snack with carne asada, maybe
23 Lode finds
24 With "in" and 25-Down, blue ribbon earner
26 Animal with a prehensile snout
28 Sand in an hourglass, for time
32 Smoke and mirrors, say
35 Nashville music mecca, for short
36 Great work
38 Comical Bruce
39 U.S. broadcaster in 40+ languages
40 It's solid blue, in pool
42 Emanation from Babel
43 Give moral guidance
45 South American monkey
46 Sonic the Hedgehog's company
47 Meat grade below "choice"
49 Club providing lots of loft
51 Coop offspring
53 With "in" and 41-Down, heir to the throne
54 Tel ___
56 Gavel wielder's word
58 Dogs with dark tongues
62 With "in" and 55-Down, use without proper respect, as a name
63 Button on an alarm clock
65 Generation ___
66 Lender's security
67 N.F.L. team with the mascot Swoop
68 With "in" and 60-Down, prepare for an ambush
69 Center of learning: Abbr.
70 Doesn't merely cut
71 Yadda yadda yadda

DOWN

1 Cry from a thrill ride
2 See 14-Across
3 Oklahoma tribesmen
4 Haul (around)
5 Astronomical altar
6 Deteriorated
7 Jedi master
8 Not yet inaugurated
9 What one might do after a firing
10 Celebrate
11 "Uncle!"
12 See 19-Across
13 Makeshift housing
21 Site that began as AuctionWeb
25 See 24-Across
27 Student grant named for a senator
28 Pulls up stakes
29 Lyric poem
30 Off-road rides
31 Apply, as lotion
33 English architect Jones
34 Tenor Ronan ___
37 Duke Ellington classic
40 Classic model train brand
41 See 53-Across
44 Impassioned
46 Jedi foes
48 Deep-sixes
50 What a gourmand eats to
52 Robert who played Mr. Chips
54 Literary Hun king
55 See 62-Across
57 Feeling sluggish
59 Get an eyeful
60 See 68-Across
61 Architect's detail, for short
64 Series ender

by Gary Cee

ACROSS
1 "Humbug" preceders
5 Gobble (down)
10 Ordered
14 Polyunsaturated fat source
15 ___-Leste (U.N. member since 2002)
16 "The Sopranos" co-star
17 Tidal movement
19 Bhagavad ___ (Hindu text)
20 Occasioned
21 "La Bamba" performers
23 Firm last words?
26 Barbara Eden title role
28 Triple, quadruple or more
29 ___-rock
30 Something Garfield often takes
32 Like some stockings
36 Popular dorm poster subject
37 Take one's licks, in a way
40 "___ been there"
41 See 26-Down
43 Triple ___
44 Small number
45 Passion
48 Fixes
51 "Be careful!"
55 "House" actor for the show's entire run
56 Lady Gaga and others
59 Brightest star in Lyra
60 How 17-, 23-, 37- and 51-Across run (in two ways)
63 Like crème brûlée
64 Some campaigns win them
65 "You Are My Destiny" singer
66 Unsupportive words
67 Hook up with
68 Accident investigator, for short

DOWN
1 Big game
2 Conditioner additive
3 Added up
4 Moderate
5 The bus stops here: Abbr.
6 Possible coup instigator, for short
7 Enjoy a constitutional
8 Men of steel?
9 San Joaquin Valley city
10 Homophobia, e.g.
11 Out
12 Get clean
13 Take marks off
18 End
22 Actress Balaban of "Last Chance Harvey"
24 Trattoria menu heading
25 It's sat upon
26 With 41-Across, co-creator of Captain America and the Hulk
27 Pre-coll., in education
31 Equipment in some labs
33 Marriage or divorce
34 Finito
35 "That's ___ to me"
37 Poet Elinor
38 Watch
39 ___-deucey
42 Gives away
46 Visage
47 Many a Sherpa
49 "If you prick ___ we not bleed?": Shak.
50 One of the so-called "Four Asian Tigers"
51 Like tapestries
52 Movado competitor
53 Disposed to henpecking
54 Actor Davis
57 Puts it to
58 Attempt
61 Stroller rider
62 General on a Chinese menu

by Julian Lim

40 MEDIUM

ACROSS

1 Sails fixed to bowsprits
5 Reform Party candidate of 1996
10 What cats often do in the spring
14 Grounded birds
15 Psychoanalyst Fromm
16 Designed for flight, for short
17 "It just can't be predicted"
20 Sermon subject
21 Vintner's dregs
22 Some farm machines
23 Puts forward as fact
25 Come-___
26 "False!"
32 2005 "Survivor" island nation
35 Guffaw syllable
36 That certain something
37 "I ___ the opinion . . ."
38 Tumbler, e.g.
40 Rules' partners, briefly
41 Massage deeply
42 An end to sex?
43 Shake hands (on)
44 "Later"
48 Exclamations of tsuris
49 How bettors may act
52 Easy to prepare, in ads
55 Part of GTO
56 French possessive
58 Work containing 21 epistles
61 Museum area
62 Tower of ___ (puzzle with pegs and rings)
63 Sister of Luke, in sci-fi
64 Muscular firmness
65 Like "The Biggest Loser" contestants
66 Sound suggested by the first letters of the words in 17-, 26-, 44- and 58-Across

DOWN

1 Movie foes of the Sharks
2 Beatnik's "Gotcha"
3 Like a well-behaved niño
4 Abbr. retired after Gorbachev's resignation
5 Pre-euro currency
6 One of the winemaking Gallos
7 Kia subcompacts
8 N.L.C.S. mo.
9 "L.A. Woman" band
10 Figure for a rep to achieve
11 Whodunit suspect, perhaps
12 Predatory seabird
13 Follows relentlessly
18 Diplomat Root
19 Post-Carnival period
24 Hangout for teachers
27 Word on Moses' tablets
28 "Illmatic" rapper
29 Sorry sort
30 Wanderlust, e.g.
31 Life of Riley
32 Reader's goal
33 Mine, to Mimi
34 Hang loose
38 Question while covering someone's eyes
39 Left Coast airport letters
43 Brand owned by Whirlpool
45 Closing bell org.
46 Some sculptures
47 Headed for sudden death, say
50 "___ bad moon rising"
51 Surround on all sides
52 Packaging abbr.
53 Louisville's river
54 Sherilyn of "Twin Peaks"
55 Blood type determinant
57 Hartford insurance company symbol
59 A patron may run one
60 Org. for Tigers, but not Lions or Bears

by Mark Bickham

ACROSS

1 Lingo suffix
4 City down the river from Florence
8 "Seriously!"
14 Accepted defeat
16 Explain in detail
17 A and others
18 Horse-drawn vehicle
19 Begin a journey
20 Took care of business
21 Shed item
22 Lines first used on a pack of Wrigley's gum: Abbr.
24 Word before "happiness," "majesty" and "fame" at the start of a Shelley poem
25 Discovers
29 They're taken in hammocks
32 Ref. with more than 2 ½ million quotations
33 It's for the birds
36 Decline
37 Like many first-time voters
41 Dante's "The Divine Comedy," e.g.
43 Return addressee?
44 Badlands sight
46 Teachers' union: Abbr.
47 Del ___ (fast-food chain)
49 Supermarket option
53 Consist of
55 Hoopster Ming
56 "___ won't!"
58 Faces
61 Where something's always brewing?
65 Relax
66 Quarrel . . . or a feature of five answers in this puzzle
67 World capital that's a setting for three Bond films
68 "See!"
69 Doc Brown in the "Back to the Future" films
70 Frosted Flakes mascot
71 Clever comment

DOWN

1 PayPal funds, e.g.
2 Kinda
3 Access card, say
4 Modest kiss
5 Lay off
6 Escort to the door
7 Some plugs
8 Santo Domingo is on one
9 Give rise to
10 Continued
11 Conquistador's quest
12 Jai ___
13 Lopsided win
15 Early second-century year
20 Kit Carson, professionally
23 Ltr. addenda
26 Former White House nickname
27 Enlarge a hole in
28 Lip
30 Big eater
31 Plant, maybe
34 Marine eagle
35 Rank
37 "___-Willow" (song from "The Mikado")
38 Unsuccessful '70s–'80s cause
39 Much film watching, e.g.
40 Awards show named for a TV network
42 Chem class may have one
45 Little battery
48 "Otherwise . . ."
50 Food named six times in a children's number rhyme
51 Assumed name
52 Kind of eyes
54 Brilliance
57 Words from one who'd rather not call?
58 Case that may be treated with cream
59 Phony
60 Promote
62 North Carolina university
63 Join (with)
64 Cleanse (of)
66 Toned

by James Tuttle

42 MEDIUM

ACROSS

1 Puerto Rican port
6 Spot on a small screen
10 The hots
14 "See ya!"
15 Super Bowl XXXIV winners
16 "Break ___ me gently"
17 Fashion designer with a signature scent
19 Way of comporting oneself
20 Thousand-mile journey, say
21 Thor's father
22 Reason to drill
23 Press on
25 "C'est magnifique!"
26 Brings to a boil?
29 Spot for a window box
31 Hangman turn
32 Singer who said "Thanks for listenin'"
36 Dame ___ Everage
37 Priests who teach the dharma
38 Novel subtitled "A Narrative of Adventures in the South Seas"
39 Part of a three-monkey phrase
41 Saw wood, so to speak
42 Piece to lounge on
43 Investment pro
44 Bulked up like a weightlifter
47 "This was ___ finest hour": Churchill
49 Rehab candidates
50 Final Four org.
51 Informal contraction
55 Rapper ___ Dogg
56 "Annie's Song" singer
58 Moreno of "West Side Story"
59 Devoted
60 Rock with bands
61 Utah Valley University city
62 Gas station freebies, once
63 Needing a massage, maybe

DOWN

1 Diplomatic goal
2 Fish market emanation
3 Like guys who finish last, per Durocher
4 Single scoop
5 Key next to F1
6 Commerce
7 Double scoop
8 Closing word
9 Broadband letters
10 Triple scoop
11 Erie Canal city
12 Make off with
13 Skater Harding
18 Brewery supply
22 They may be measured by the pound
24 ___ Smith's Pies
25 Works of Horace
26 Yellows or grays, say
27 Like some sunbathers
28 Pulitzer-winning journalist Weingarten
30 Bibliography abbr.
32 Polynesian beverage
33 "Everything's fine, thanks"
34 Drove like mad
35 Many a gardener at work
37 Tax
40 Traditional paintings
41 ___ Lanka
43 Necklace piece
44 Saki's real surname
45 Carrier name until 1997
46 Number of hills of Roma
48 Analog clock features
50 PBS science series
52 Author Turgenev
53 Brooklyn team since 2012
54 ___-hugger
56 Improvise, as a band
57 "___ my shorts!": Bart Simpson

by Todd Gross

ACROSS

1 Rowdydow
4 Its logo's letters have a stripe running through them
8 2004 sci-fi film based on a 1950 book
14 Fix
15 African healer
16 Eerie phenomenon
17 *Some vacation travel
19 Atom who directed "The Sweet Hereafter"
20 90° from N?
21 Say inaudibly
23 Flamenco shout
24 Border
26 Will certainly receive
28 Tay and Fyne
31 "Toddlers & Tiaras" airer
33 Cream ___
34 Loan letters
35 Nicole Polizzi, familiarly
38 Toned
40 Place to gambol
41 *Caboose
43 Long in Hollywood
44 Start of many a tale
46 English word derived from Tswana
47 Seventh-century start
48 ___-Lo ("I Wish" rapper)
50 ___ equivalent (measure of explosive energy)
51 Chicken for a chicken dinner
53 Flips
55 Palindromic emperor
57 Birth control option, briefly
58 He wrote "Hell is other people"
60 Mauna ___
63 Acts the curmudgeon
65 2012 software release . . . or a hint to the starts of the answers to the starred clues
68 Understood by few
69 Axe target?
70 Fraternity character
71 Pint-size
72 Next word after "Wherefore art thou Romeo?"
73 Not too smart

DOWN

1 Tangent starter?
2 "Bad Teacher" star, 2011
3 "Hop-o'-My-Thumb" figure
4 Mr. Potato Head piece
5 Virginia ___
6 *What makes bread rise?
7 Natural hatchery
8 ___ fixes
9 Fix, in a way, as golf clubs
10 Eye, south of the border
11 *Area with the world's highest tides
12 *Bushes were once found there
13 One concerned with pitches
18 Virginia ___
22 *1965 hit that ends "My baby don't care"
25 Apt anagram of "Russ."
27 Small lump
28 French composer Édouard
29 *Like Linux
30 *Frozen daiquiri ingredient
32 "The Millionairess" star, 1960
36 Rim attachment
37 Trade-___
39 50-50, say
42 Nimble
45 Certain M.I.T. grads
49 Gallery supporters?
52 Hershey brand
53 Political commentator Paul
54 Sickly pale
56 Dovetail joint part
59 Like most movies
61 Was behind, in a way
62 Palazzo Alfieri's locale
64 "Poultry in motion," e.g.
66 Like claret
67 Rush-hour hour

by David Steinberg

44 MEDIUM

ACROSS

1 Hasbro action figure
6 Pile up
11 Excite, with "up"
14 Grenoble's river
15 One of the "Honeymooners"
16 Whom a guy do-si-dos with
17 Face value?
19 Detergent name
20 Org. with launch parties?
21 Dissection class
23 Blind as ___
25 Face value?
28 Nancy Drew findings
30 Some Monopoly properties: Abbr.
31 Home of Cherokee Natl. Forest
32 ___ clip (bike attachment)
33 Reason to cram
35 Viejo : Sp. :: ___ : Ger.
37 Face value?
42 Like the Triple Word Score squares in Scrabble
43 Look at the stars, say
44 Airport alternative to JFK
46 ___ buco
49 Lobster catcher
50 Boot camp routine
52 Face value?
56 Many Monopoly properties: Abbr.
57 Virginia's Luray ___
58 Scale amount
60 HI-strung instrument?
61 Face value?
66 Stew tidbit
67 Eskimo
68 Place for a coatrack
69 Abbr. before "truly"
70 Where Hercules slew a lion
71 Stellar grade

DOWN

1 Alternative to .jpg
2 Acre's locale: Abbr.
3 "Earth's Children" author
4 Like Rococo architecture
5 Cartoon squeals
6 D-backs, in box scores
7 Playing piece
8 Cover stories
9 Give away, as a movie ending
10 "I'm all ears!"
11 Time of first steps, often
12 Place to doodle
13 Not stop a musical gig
18 "Well, ___-di-dah"
22 Game with a multiplier
23 Comport oneself
24 Soviet ___
26 ___ Sea (greatly shrunken body of water)
27 Toon voiced by Jim Backus
29 Golf's Ballesteros
34 Marked wrong
35 Wood-shaping tool
36 Perjured oneself
38 Jagged, as a leaf's edge
39 Grp. whose initials in French are the reverse of its English initials
40 Toon with size 14-AAAAAA shoes
41 Check the figures?
45 Two of racing's Unsers
46 Modern protest name
47 Salt or pepper holder
48 Computer command under "File"
49 Woods critter
51 Convertible, in slang
53 Gen. Rommel, the Desert Fox
54 Cockamamie
55 Part of B.Y.O.B.
59 Big name in photography, once
62 Rush
63 "Give ___ rest!"
64 Opposite of 35-Across
65 Org. in a 2013 scandal

by Richard F. Mausser

ACROSS

1 Start of a word ladder whose first and last words are suggested by 36-Across
5 Ladder, part 2
9 Ladder, part 3
13 Enya's homeland
14 "___ fool . . ."
15 Roberts of NPR
16 Degrees for foreign attys.
17 Yoga equipment
18 Wolf in Kipling's "The Jungle Book"
19 South American tuber
20 Verdi's "___ nome"
21 Norse love goddess
22 Via ___ (main street in ancient Rome)
24 Ladder, part 4
26 Good baseball hit: Abbr.
28 Suppress
31 Still in the oven, say
33 Abstainer
35 Luau strings
36 Lucky lotto participant
39 Place for a skateboarder's pad
40 Worked, in a way
41 "Personally . . ."
43 Eli
47 Mark, as a ballot square
48 Ladder, part 5
50 Nikon alternative
51 Bother persistently
53 Commuter's destination, often
56 Like 1-Down: Abbr.
57 Tried to nip
58 Home to Andrew Wyeth's "Christina's World," informally
59 ___ bene
60 Jonathan Swift's "___ of a Tub"
61 Melodramatic cry
62 Lit ___
63 Ladder, part 6
64 Ladder, part 7
65 End of the word ladder

DOWN

1 House speaker after Hastert
2 Tin Man's need
3 Jerry of "Law & Order"
4 Thing in court
5 Fine grade of cotton
6 "While you live, / Drink!" poet
7 Leading
8 ___ Gatos, Calif.
9 Prod
10 "Fine by me"
11 Cartoon character on the 3/31/52 cover of Life magazine
12 Rustic setting
15 Addition mark
20 Venetian explorer John
21 Home of Cocoa Beach
23 Salon worker, at times
25 Like some streets and tickets
27 French article
29 Tightly tied, say
30 Ant farm feature
32 Scottish port on the Firth of Tay
34 Canonized Fr. woman
36 Nissan make
37 Kind of ward
38 Rapper with the 2002 #1 hit "Hot in Herre"
39 Crunchy breakfast bowlful
42 Speak to the Senate, say
44 Olympic skater Ito
45 ___ acid
46 Broadway Joe
49 Dangerous breakout
52 8 on the Beaufort scale
54 Apple variety
55 Zap, in a way
57 Cheers, on TV
58 Spoil
59 Big maker of A.T.M.'s

by Elizabeth C. Gorski

46 MEDIUM

ACROSS

1 "Per aspera ad ___"
6 Big throw
11 Creamy concoction
14 Joy, formerly of "The View"
15 Slightly off balance
16 Magnetite or cinnabar
17 Result of someone yelling "Fire!" in a crowded theater?
19 Starfish appendage
20 Sam of "Jurassic Park"
21 They might be manicured
23 "That's revolting!"
25 Looting of a legislature?
29 Laker legend Bryant
31 Skin-and-bones
32 Salon employee
33 Drink that cures all ills
36 Skirt
38 83, for the creators of this puzzle . . . or a hint to the ends of 17-, 25-, 51- and 60-Across
42 Blue Grotto locale
43 Spanish charger
45 Belle's caller
48 O.K. Corral lawman
50 "Idylls of the King" woman
51 What an exploding microwave can make?
55 What follows a bee?
56 Survey option
57 Prop in "Snow White and the Seven Dwarfs"
59 0
60 Exemption from playing an instrument at school?
66 Dander
67 Cain's eldest son
68 Home unlikely to have air-conditioning
69 Six-time All-Star Ron
70 Beardless dwarf
71 Scrumptious

DOWN

1 Five simoleons
2 Number between quinque and septem
3 Be a dreamer
4 Evaluate
5 Secret alternative
6 Source of the saying "Brevity is the soul of wit"
7 Skill at picking things up?
8 Letters between names
9 Chillax, with "out"
10 Tom of "The Seven Year Itch"
11 Winter Olympics powerhouse
12 County name in California, Florida and New York
13 One blowing off steam
18 Iran's ___ Khamenei
22 Pasta preference
23 Onetime White House nickname
24 Common part of a Happy Meal
26 1993 Tom Cruise legal thriller
27 Carpet surface
28 Toughen
30 Carry out
34 Home of the Salmon River Mtns.
35 Mature
37 Corona ___ Mar, Calif.
39 Beer bash venue
40 Palms, e.g.
41 1813's Battle of Lake ___
44 Ben Jonson wrote one "to Himself"
45 Not quite human, maybe
46 Whole
47 Benson of "Pretty Little Liars"
49 Keen
52 Ready for a duel, say
53 Apt rhyme of "aah"
54 Bowler's woe
58 Women drivers' grp.
61 Colorful card game
62 Soak (up)
63 Winter coat?
64 Bar fixture
65 ___ milk

by David Steinberg (16) and Bernice Gordon (99)

ACROSS

1 Kind of muffin
5 Apple grower?
11 Interject
14 Wagon trails have them
15 Boy who pulls the sword from the stone in "The Sword in the Stone"
16 Barack Obama, for one
17 Women's soccer star Wambach
18 Oceanus and Hyperion
19 ___ Search (former name for Bing)
20 California ballplayer's pound?
22 "A fickle food," to Emily Dickinson
23 Stadium recorder
24 Día de los Santos Reyes month
26 Missouri ballplayer's connection?
31 Baby's word
35 Around
36 Texas city that's headquarters for J. C. Penney
37 Actors Ken and Lena
39 Rap sheet abbr.
40 Corporate department
41 Band with the 1984 hit "My Oh My"
42 Fires
44 Junk mail encl., sometimes
45 Michigan ballplayer's rubbish?
48 Total mess
49 "Time is money" and others
54 Tae ___ do
55 Pennsylvania ballplayer's joint?
59 Gaming inits.
60 The Penguin's player in "Batman Returns"
61 There may be one for "8 items or less"
62 "The Book of ___" (2010 film)
63 1974 foreign-language hit
64 Sons of ___ (ethnic pride group)
65 Trains in Chicago
66 Out
67 Trial balloon

DOWN

1 Crows
2 Father of a 1980s craze
3 Held in check
4 Popular quintet that included two former Mouseketeers
5 Cricket player
6 La Salle of "Coming to America"
7 Aleutian island
8 Spicy cuisine
9 Joan who once co-hosted "Good Morning America"
10 Hosp. units
11 One way to prepare pollo
12 Where Ronald Reagan worked as a sports announcer
13 Ready to serve
21 Washington's Sea-___ Airport
22 Guys
25 Drops off, maybe
27 Not take it lying down
28 Westernmost city on the African mainland
29 Hassan Rowhani, for one
30 Bad thing to pick
31 Biblical verb
32 "No problems here"
33 Result of an exam
34 Like vicuñas
38 One doing the lord's work
43 Said quickly
46 Top-notch
47 Program file suffix
50 Exposed sandbar, maybe
51 Airport named for a naval war hero
52 Some BMW vehicles
53 Tuckered out
54 Attack at close range, maybe
56 Composer Charles
57 Knoll
58 Memo abbr.
60 Justice Department div.

by Sean Dobbin

48 MEDIUM

ACROSS

1 Long part of a lance
6 Radar screen dot
10 ___-à-porter
14 Actor Quinn
15 Charlie Chaplin's last wife
16 Singsong syllables
17 What Ali Baba found on the treasure in the cave?
20 In the mail
21 Heart of the matter
22 Simple
23 Not supportin'
25 Down Under runners
27 Sign of a failed practice?
33 Baseball exec Bud
34 ___ trap
35 Honour bestowed by Queen Elizabeth: Abbr.
36 Sch. near Beverly Hills
37 Letter closing
39 Bar from Mars
40 Avril follower
41 Grammy-winning blues guitarist Jonny
42 In need of some manscaping, say
43 Puzzles as gifts?
47 Website that users themselves may revise
48 Many a Rolling Stone cover subject
49 You'll need to take steps to get to it
52 ___ sci
54 Lerner & Loewe musical set in Paris
58 Be startled by singing monks?
61 Suit to ___
62 ___ dire (court examination)
63 Seat for a stand-up
64 Coloratura's practice
65 1990s compacts
66 What a verb ending may indicate

DOWN

1 Suckers
2 Employ
3 Deuce follower
4 1940 Disney film
5 Big bang letters
6 Sound of disgust
7 Digs in an old warehouse, maybe
8 Prevalent, as a rumor
9 Sound of disgust
10 When repeated several times, child's entreaty
11 Sitar master Shankar
12 Stat for 26-Down: Abbr.
13 Stun with a charge
18 Option on "Wheel of Fortune"
19 Arctic language
24 Booking
26 Cascades, e.g.: Abbr.
27 Old Renault
28 Stan's film partner
29 Toupee alternative
30 Lose-lose
31 Car mentioned in the Beach Boys' "Fun, Fun, Fun"
32 Hot, like a hunk
33 Cesspool
37 American, in England
38 Moving stealthily
39 Party in the parking lot
41 Classic shooter
42 Med. care option
44 Acquires with sticky fingers
45 Crude fleet
46 Guarantor of financial accts.
49 Open a crack
50 Hippo's wear in 4-Down
51 Eliot Ness and others
53 Home of Miami University
55 Wise to
56 Classic muscle cars
57 Archipelago part
59 "The whole family can watch" program rating
60 33rd president's monogram

by Paula Gamache

ACROSS

1 ___ skirt
5 "The Tao of Pooh" author Benjamin
9 One with ergophobia
14 "Look what I found!" cries
15 Kind of tradition
16 "___ talk?"
17 "Good thing I don't have the same problem!"
19 Following
20 River of film
21 1986 top 10 hit for Billy Idol
23 That's the point
24 Meal at which to drink four cups of wine
25 Part of a pickup line?
28 "___, boy!"
29 Earth goddess created by Chaos
33 Expanse
36 "Apparently"
38 What fell in the Fall
39 That is the question
41 Robert of "Quincy, M.E."
42 One who may need a shower?
44 Holder of a pair of queens
46 Shiner
47 Milk sources
49 N.B.A. Hall-of-Famer Walker
50 Belgian battleground during W.W. I
52 Letters in car ads
54 "Truthfully . . ."
57 Brought up to speed
61 Yokel, in slang
62 Classic rock song in "Easy Rider"
64 G.W. competitor
65 P.D.Q. Bach's "I'm the Village Idiot," e.g.
66 Rep. Darrell of California
67 Like the myth of Ragnarok
68 Luxury hotel name
69 Locale for a Village People hit, informally

DOWN

1 "Scrubs" locale: Abbr.
2 "Don't even think about it"
3 Bats
4 Showed politeness at the front door
5 Certain ring bearer
6 Relative of a gemsbok
7 ___ Schwarz
8 Fictional substance in a Disney film
9 Zodiac symbol
10 U.S.S. Enterprise chief engineer Geordi ___
11 Where reruns run
12 Overly precious
13 Mister, overseas
18 ___ Balls
22 Christmas hymn beginning
24 Events at which people are dead serious?
25 Some pyramids
26 In two, say
27 Ohio city WSW of Columbus
28 It's possessive
30 Some buggy drivers
31 Name on a bottle of Sensuous Nude perfume
32 Half of an old comedy team
34 Caen cleric
35 Butch Cassidy and the Sundance Kid, e.g.
37 Drifts away
40 Quaker product
43 Chardonnay feature
45 "Whatever!"
48 Fancy suite amenity
51 In and of itself
52 Ball mate
53 Mr. ___
54 What's not for big shots?
55 38-Across's genus
56 "Ah, my Beloved, fill the Cup that clears" poet
57 "I say" sayer
58 Menu section
59 Threat ender
60 Time of 1944's Operation Neptune
63 ". . . goes, ___ go!"

by Evan Birnholz

50 MEDIUM

ACROSS

1 Exposure units
5 Like many a superhero
10 Cheater's sound, maybe
14 Biblical twin
15 First in a line of Russian grand princes
16 Jazzy James
17 & 20 Story by 42-Across on which the movie "Blade Runner" is based
21 Best-suited for a job
22 Kind of lily
23 Cold war foe, slangily
26 Cause of a dramatic death in Shakespeare
27 Go ballistic
28 Displace
31 Music magazine founded by Bob Guccione Jr.
35 Disloyal sort
36 Like bits of old music in some new music
39 Keats creation
40 One going for a little bite?
42 Author Philip K. ___
43 XXX
45 Cleanse
47 Auctioned investments, in brief
48 Affright
51 Eat, eat, eat
54 & 59 Story by 42-Across on which the movie "Total Recall" is based
60 Together, in Toulouse
61 Swiss miss of fiction
62 African antelope
63 "Shane" star Alan
64 Put back in the fold
65 "Gnarly!"

DOWN

1 Request after a failure, sometimes
2 Since
3 Christine ___, heroine of "The Phantom of the Opera"
4 Light that darkens
5 Club
6 "Let's take ___"
7 Competition category in bridge and skating
8 Break off a relationship
9 Kind of brake
10 Noncommittal response
11 Andrew Carnegie's industry
12 Author Madame de ___
13 Home of the N.H.L.'s Lightning
18 Accountants put them on the left
19 Mil. awards
23 Humorist Bennett
24 Like some contraceptives
25 Remote button
26 Bruiser
28 Ascap rival
29 It's scanned in a store, for short
30 U2 song paying tribute to an American icon
32 Sulk
33 Run while standing still
34 Takes home
37 Throw in
38 View from Budapest
41 Ready for battle
44 Cares for maybe too much
46 "___ expert, but . . ."
47 "One ringy-dingy" comic
48 Ghastly
49 "Bleeding Love" singer Lewis
50 Astringent
51 Bird that's as small as it sounds
52 Beatnik's "Gotcha"
53 Sparkly rock
55 Essen's river
56 Like hurricanes in January
57 Three-time N.H.L. All-Star Kovalchuk
58 "u r so funny . . . lmao," e.g.

by Jason Flinn

ACROSS

1 Common catch off the coast of Maryland
9 Light, in a way
15 Crude alternative
16 Jewelry box item
17 Like a bout on an undercard
18 Dickens's Miss Havisham, famously
19 ID clincher
20 Challenge to ambulance chasers
22 Arcade game prize grabber
24 Fiacre, to taxi drivers
27 "___ reminder . . ."
30 Nook occupier
31 Toshiba competitor
32 Some camcorders
33 Besmirch
36 Isaac Bashevis Singer settings
38 Culmination
39 Only proper noun in the Beatles' "Revolution"
41 "Something to Talk About" singer, 1991
42 Golf commentator's subject
43 Classic kitschy wall hanging
46 Slip for a skirt?
47 "Billy Bathgate" novelist
50 Ex-G.I.'s org.
53 Washington State mascot
54 Pre-W.W. I in automotive history
57 "If music be the food of love . . ." speaker in "Twelfth Night"
58 Cry of despair
59 Nothing: It.
60 Periods of warming . . . or cooling off

DOWN

1 M asset
2 Royal Arms of England symbol
3 Bone under a watchband
4 The Orange Bowl is played on it: Abbr.
5 Acupuncturist's concern
6 Croupier's stick material
7 Acknowledges
8 Tab carrier in a bar?
9 Tourist attraction on Texas' Pedernales River
10 Face in a particular direction
11 "Champagne for One" sleuth
12 Shot, informally
13 Serena Williams, often
14 Novel in Joyce Carol Oates's Wonderland Quartet
21 Exasperates
22 Cauldron stirrer
23 "The Avengers" villain, 2012
24 Bit of sachet stuffing
25 Classroom clickers of old
26 Singer who once sang a song to Kramer on "Seinfeld"
27 When "Ave Maria" is sung in "Otello"
28 1970s pact partly negotiated in Helsinki
29 Right hands: Abbr.
32 Arena
34 Orange garnish for a sushi roll
35 Fox hunt cry
37 Bay, for one
40 Prompt a buzzer on "The Price Is Right"
43 Unoccupied
44 Massive, in Metz
45 Block
46 Keep from taking off, as a plane with low visibility
47 Nobel category: Abbr.
48 Loughlin or Petty of Hollywood
49 Italian actress Eleonora
50 Let it all out
51 Unoccupied
52 Rolls of dough
55 One of the Ms. Pac-Man ghosts
56 "There is no ___ except stupidity": Wilde

by Brad Wilber

52 HARD

ACROSS

1 Insignificant row
9 Traffic reporter's aid
15 Big rush, maybe
16 Twin's rival
17 Offerer of stock advice
18 Grown-up who's not quite grown up
19 No big shot?
20 Nasty intentions
22 Threatening word
23 Overseas rebellion cry
25 One may be played by a geisha
26 Wasn't given a choice
27 "You Be ___" (1986 hip-hop hit)
29 Super German?
31 Pressure
33 Launch site
34 Where many airways are cleared, briefly
35 Antithesis of 32-Down
37 Common sound in Amish country
39 Large amount
42 Classics with 389 engines
44 Scrammed
48 Like Fabergé eggs
51 Schoolyard retort
52 Carry ___
53 So great
55 Paving block
56 Golf lesson topic
57 Goes downhill
59 Troubling post-engagement status, briefly
60 Doctor
62 They were labeled "Breakfast," "Dinner" and "Supper"
64 2002 César winner for Best Film
65 Real rubbish
66 Least significant
67 It really gets under your skin

DOWN

1 Determine the value of freedom?
2 Carp
3 Scandinavia's oldest university
4 Sneeze lead-ins
5 Austrian conductor Karl
6 Recess
7 Be quiet, say
8 Savor the flattery
9 It's bad when nobody gets it
10 "The Guilt Trip" actress Graynor
11 Like some cartilage piercings
12 "Possibly"
13 Dream team member
14 Planet threateners
21 Like a top
24 Stain producers
26 Gallant
28 Result of knuckling down?
30 Hollow
32 Antithesis of 35-Across
36 Pageant judging criterion
38 Ed supporters
39 Park Avenue's ___ Building
40 Radical
41 Shaking
43 Sniffing a lot
45 What a slightly shy person may request
46 1967 Emmy winner for playing Socrates
47 "As you like it" phrase
49 What a bunch of footballers might do
50 Game in which the lowest card is 7
54 Marriott rival
57 Preventer of many bites
58 Bit of action
61 Household name?
63 Soreness

by Tom Heilman

ACROSS

1 African city of 4+ million whose name means, literally, "haven of peace"
12 Seeing things
14 "Why such a fuss?"
16 Start of a Jewish holiday?
17 Put one's two cents in?
18 Arizona's Agua ___ River
19 Not natural for
21 Like Beethoven's Piano Sonata No. 6 or 22
24 Tilting figure: Abbr.
25 ___ Ximénez (dessert sherry)
26 Manipulative health care worker
29 Smash letters
30 Destroy, informally
32 Range ridges
33 Classified
35 Eatery where the Tony Award was born
38 Pitch
39 Juan's "Hey!"
42 Perseveres
44 Some Deco pieces
46 Lead film festival characters?
47 Rhineland Campaign's arena: Abbr.
48 Frito-Lay snack
50 Silver of fivethirtyeight.com
52 California city near Fullerton
54 Author Janowitz
55 Opening line of a 1966 #1 Beatles hit
59 One-hit wonder
60 Events for some antiquers

DOWN

1 Demonstration exhortation
2 A bee might light on it
3 Some N.F.L.'ers
4 Irritate
5 Dopes
6 Restoration notation
7 Even though
8 Polynesian island chain?
9 Lee with an Oscar
10 Home row sequence
11 Kalahari Desert dweller
12 Irritability
13 Femme canonisée
14 Deli menu subheading
15 Foundation for some roofing
20 Silence
22 Verges on
23 Anticipate
27 Mind
28 Irritable state
31 Election surprise
33 What some bombs result in, in brief
34 Fanciful notions
35 Dead
36 Pair of boxers?
37 Give a makeover
39 Pontiac and others
40 "Star Trek" extra
41 It's definitely not the short answer
43 "That's that"
45 Fix a key problem?
49 Kind of yoga
51 Important info for people with connections
53 Clément with two Oscar-winning films
56 Düsseldorf direction
57 La la lead-in
58 Allen of play-by-play

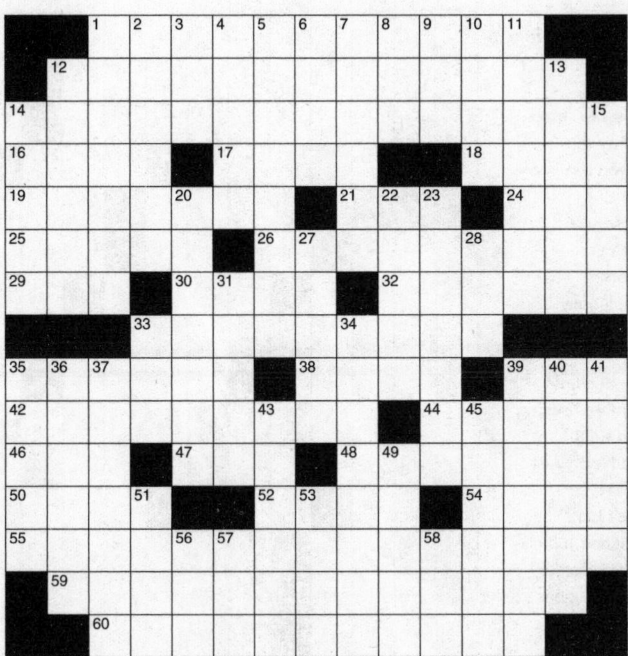

by Alan Arbesfeld

54 HARD

ACROSS

1 Made a seat-of-the-pants error?
11 "Your mama wears army boots," e.g.
15 Rioting
16 Popular pizza place, informally
17 Washington, D.C., has a famous one
18 Greets enthusiastically, in a way
19 One working in a corner in an office?
20 Eastern Woodlands native
22 Noted eavesdropper, for short
23 Covenants
25 Splendiferous
27 Bar supply
30 ___ Valley
31 Sulky
32 Tandoori-baked fare
34 "Yes" to an invitation
36 One way to stand
37 They may result when you run into people
40 Hognose snake
41 Of two minds
42 ___ work
43 Lender, legally speaking
45 Lo ___
47 50% nonunion?
48 "Gunsmoke" setting
49 Marina sight
51 Classic Northwest brewski
52 Charlie's land
54 Like a tennis match without a break?
58 Like many a gen.
60 Mother of Andromeda
62 "Iliad" locale
63 Settles in, say
64 Job application info, for short
65 Nootropics, more familiarly

DOWN

1 Internet prowlers
2 Hand or foot
3 Cry frequently made with jazz hands
4 Georg von ___
5 Vice president after whom a U.S. city is thought to have been named
6 Ninny
7 Best Picture of 1960, with "The"
8 ___ Palmas
9 Breastplate of Athena
10 "The High One"
11 Where a canine sits?
12 Whole
13 Winter Olympics sight
14 They use blue books
21 TV show headed by a former writer for "S.N.L."
24 "Mom" and "Mama's Family"
26 Poetic expanses
27 Grumpy
28 They use Blue Books
29 "The Wishing-Chair" series creator
33 Manage
35 Whiner, of a sort
38 Kind of compressor
39 Yankee, once
44 Passes
46 "Uh-uh!"
50 #2 pop
53 Title with an apostrophe
55 Appear stunned
56 Apothecary item
57 Din-din
59 Prefix with peptic
61 2 Tone influence

by Michael Ashley

ACROSS

1 Singer's tongue
8 Fast delivery
15 First name in online news
16 Detox, say
17 Autobiographical book by Carrie Fisher
19 As one
20 D.M.V. offerings
21 Peace Nobelist Kim ___-jung
22 Crispy Twister offerer
24 Peace Nobelist Hammarskjöld
25 Papua New Guinea port in W.W. II news
28 "That's nice"
30 Dept. of Labor division
34 Unit of online popularity
39 "Almost there!"
40 Nice thing to hit
41 First card played in the game parliament
43 British submachine gun
44 Bog
45 Grade sch. class
46 Badge holder: Abbr.
49 Back
51 Ermine, e.g.
54 Kind of cable in TV production
58 Actress Ryder
61 Oscar-nominated Woody Allen film
63 Mythological sister of 66-Across
64 Regardless of
65 Formidable foes
66 Mythological brother of 63-Across

DOWN

1 Went off course, as a ship
2 One of Chekhov's "Three Sisters"
3 Not accept
4 Children's author who created Miss Trunchbull
5 Scoop contents
6 Approached slyly, with "up"
7 1968 space movie villain
8 D. W. Griffith's "___ for Help"
9 "Yeah, you got me"
10 ___-car
11 Fulfill
12 Spanish liqueur
13 "___ it?"
14 Staying power
18 Cappuccino choice
23 Not soon at all
26 Who's there
27 ___ blue (color named for a school)
29 ___ for the best
31 Be hanged after a crime
32 Throng
33 Fine things?
34 Chuck
35 N.Y.C.'s PBS station
36 Big head
37 A.L. West team, on scoreboards
38 ___ disease
42 Passed out
47 Stage directions
48 Feline in un jardin zoologique
50 Major League Baseball V.I.P.
52 Merge
53 Demolishes, in Devon
54 Govt. gangbusters
55 Put out
56 Ditto, in footnotes
57 Pupil reactions
59 ___ dixit
60 Short breaks, of a sort
62 It may be said with a raised hand

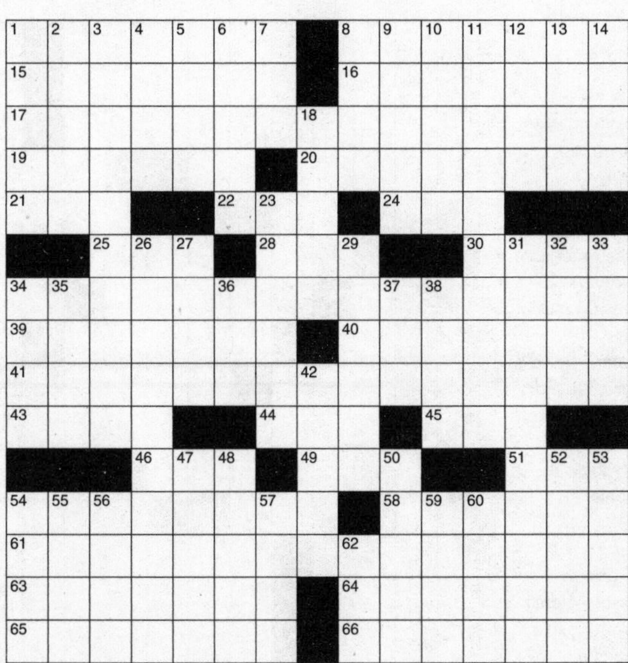

by David Kwong

56 HARD

ACROSS

1 "Good point"
11 Right hand: Abbr.
15 Yarn suppliers?
16 What severe cuts may result in, briefly
17 Lacking in drawing power?
18 Succumb to interrogation
19 Roughly half of all N.B.A. M.V.P.'s
20 Will Rogers props
22 Flavoring compound
23 Resident of Angola, Brazil or Lebanon
25 Ne'er-do-well who stayed out for a long time?
29 Vader, in his boyhood
32 Mulberry cousin
33 It's marked way down
34 Sweet-tempered type
36 Argue
38 Sylvia of jazz
39 For the stated value
41 Something to believe in
43 Getaway destination
44 #5 of the American Film Institute's all-time top 100 movie villains
47 Composer who said "Give me a laundry list and I'll set it to music"
48 U.S. city that's a girl's name
52 Hole
53 Boost
55 "Alias" actress
56 Creator of Wildfell Hall
59 Different
60 Law still in effect but no longer enforced
61 Mr. ___ (moniker for Andrei Gromyko)
62 Show with a peanut gallery

DOWN

1 Twinkling
2 Waistband brand
3 "Impossible"
4 Many a laundromat patron
5 Stopgap
6 Move around
7 Angel Clare's wife, in literature
8 Groovy track?
9 Altdorf is its capital
10 What money may be placed in
11 Stigmas
12 Quaint toe clamp tighteners
13 Green light?
14 Sounds of admonishment
21 Cow-horned deity
23 Swiss alternative
24 "Almost there . . ."
26 Super ___
27 Planet destroyed in 2009's "Star Trek"
28 Jewelry designer Peretti
29 Chiropractor on "Two and a Half Men"
30 "Of course!"
31 Be a make-up artist?
35 Where a new delivery may be placed?
37 Villain's sinister syllable
40 Ubiquitous prescription
42 Like items on Christmas lists
45 Setting of King Fahd Road
46 Fireflite of the 1950s, e.g.
49 Measures taken slowly?
50 Quiet and soft
51 Impressionism?
52 Either "True Grit" director
53 "Tennessee Waltz" lyricist ___ Stewart
54 Without fumbling
57 Con's opening?
58 Hick's nix

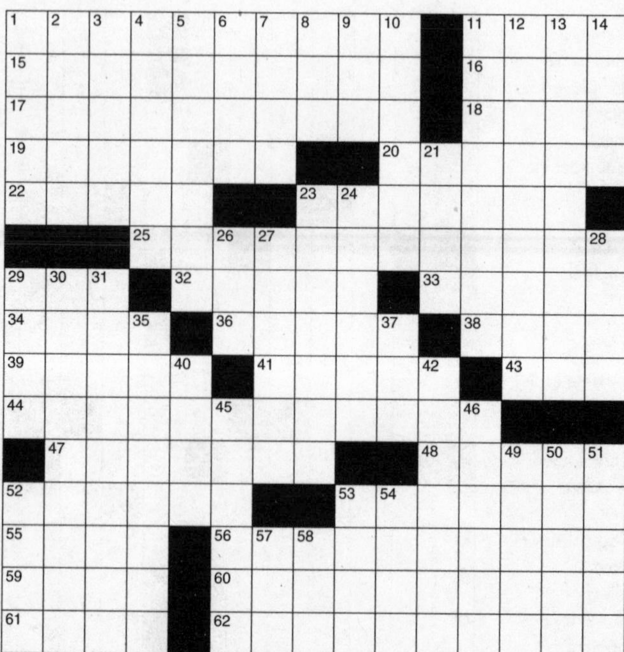

by Doug Peterson and Brad Wilber

ACROSS

1 Finish differently, say
8 1950s backup group with four top 10 hits
14 Stars are recognized with them
17 Clear as mud, so to speak
18 It may have pop-ups
19 Scott who co-starred on TV's "Men of a Certain Age"
20 "Incredible!"
21 Not just surmise
23 Closest to zero
24 Years, in Tours
26 Oakland daily, for short
28 "Unfortunately . . ."
29 Deutschland "de"
31 Phoenix setting: Abbr.
33 D.C. nine
35 It has short shortstops
41 "What, no more?"
42 Places for a 35-Across
43 ___ other (matchlessly)
44 Satyajit Ray's "The ___ Trilogy"
45 Bill in a bow tie
46 Tarantula hawk, e.g.
49 Band options
51 DreamWorks ___
53 Phoenix setting?
55 Jacuzzi session
57 "___ of Varnish" (C. P. Snow novel)
61 Chemistry test topic
63 Cursorily
65 Certain Mexican-American
66 Where to come to grips with things?
67 Tight
68 Purports

DOWN

1 Looking up
2 This, in Tijuana
3 Trash hauler
4 Much-filmed swinger
5 Ancient Dravidian's displacer
6 Like Chopin's Mazurka Op. 56 No. 1
7 Sony Reader competitor
8 Middle ear?
9 It's often set in a ring
10 Serve well in court
11 Come to
12 Hometown of the band Hanson
13 Party prizes?
15 "Shh! It's a secret!"
16 Hershey bar
22 Brogue feature
25 "The Moldau" composer
27 Mies van der Rohe was its last director
29 Something needing a stamp
30 Giant giant's family
32 "Giant" events
34 Be overrun
35 Party label for Brit. P.M. William Gladstone
36 Culture centers?
37 Chuck Schumer's predecessor in the Senate
38 Kids' rhyme starter
39 Congress person
40 Works for an editor: Abbr.
46 Takes orders, say
47 Concern of I.R.S. Form 8594
48 Japanese sliding door
50 Head makeup
52 Superman's name on Krypton
54 Hong Kong's Hang ___ Index
56 Polynesian drink
58 Pull felt on Earth
59 Part of a French play
60 Cher's role in "Burlesque"
62 "The Natural" hero Hobbs
64 Former Mets manager Hodges

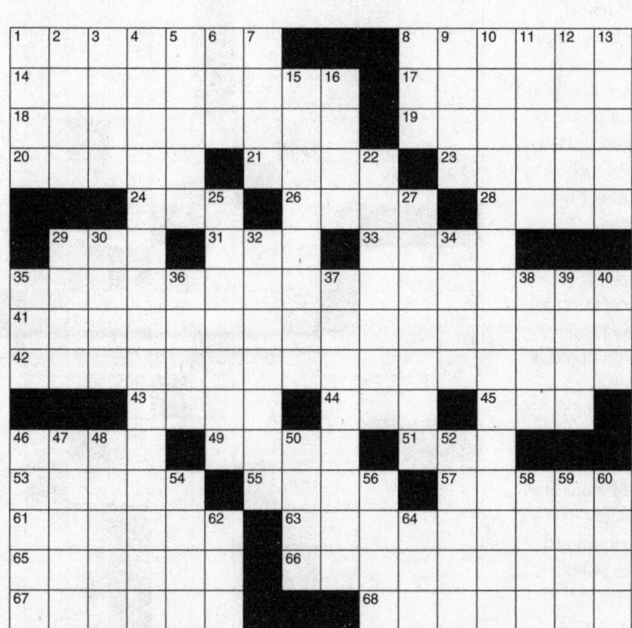

by Derek Bowman

58 HARD

ACROSS

1 Chest piece
7 St. John's, for one
15 Fish that attaches itself to a host
16 Like the Congressional Record
17 Biblical prophet whose name means "Yahweh is my God"
18 Act in "The Last Samurai"
19 St. John's, for one
20 Kneecap, e.g.
22 Dick and Al, recently
23 Like King Sargon II: Abbr.
25 33-Down*
27 Author of "Herding Cats: A Life in Politics"
29 Latin rock band featured at Woodstock
33 Where the guarani is cash
37 Milk source, to a kid
38 Vein gloriousness?
39 Pope who started the First Crusade
41 Tokyo Rose's real first name
42 German chocolate brand
44 Good occasion for kite-flying
46 Shows an aptitude for
48 Mother of the Titans
49 32-Down*
51 Home of more than 900 volcanoes
55 White House girl
58 Western setting
60 Just under half a penny's weight
61 Place
63 Ostrich, e.g.
65 1950s H-bomb test site
66 Dermatological concern
67 Classic graduation gifts
68 The Missouri, to the Mississippi

DOWN

1 ___ blank
2 Transfers often entail them, informally
3 Bahrain bigwigs: Var.
4 John Paul II, originally
5 Span of a ruler, maybe
6 First name in Chicago politics
7 Part of the coast of Brazil
8 Estée Lauder fragrance for men
9 TV or monitor part: Abbr.
10 "Beats me!"
11 Did with enjoyment
12 Ellington band vocalist Anderson
13 68-Across*
14 Father/daughter fighters
21 Take ___ at
24 Iran, North Korea and the like
26 Veneer, e.g.
28 Ask, as for assistance
30 It's not basic
31 Astronomical figure?
32 Out
33 Strong wine
34 "La donna è mobile," e.g.
35 Give off, with "of"
36 Not pitch or roll, say
40 Big uranium exporter
43 Twin-engine Navy helicopter
45 Site of the Three Gorges Dam
47 Hoofing it
50 Abruptly stops, with "out"
52 Like mummies
53 Instruction written in currants for Alice
54 Campaign dirty trick
55 Coast, in a way
56 1-Across*
57 Univ. grouping
59 Nonkosher
62 Samson's end?
64 Pal

* *taking into account its 61-Across*

by Matt Ginsberg

ACROSS

1 Closer to the edge, say
8 Brothers' keepers?
14 Summer time eponym
16 Peso : Mexico :: ___ : Panama
17 "NYC 22" replaced it in 2012
18 Key represented by all white keys on a piano
19 Plate holder
20 Kin of clubs
22 Sporty Spice, by another name
23 Hernando's "Hey!"
24 Batcave, e.g.
25 End point of a common journey
26 Ginnie ___
28 Darling
30 Univ. figures
31 Style of New York's Sony Building
34 '60s film character wearing one black glove
35 Literary classic featuring the teen Tadzio
36 Teen "Whoa!"
37 Grp. concerned with violence levels
38 With 43-Across, part of a squid
39 Long-running Mell Lazarus comic strip
41 What you may squeal with
43 See 38-Across
46 "Think of ___ . . ."
47 Dipped
48 Biblical waste?
50 Run one's mouth
52 Allowing no equivocation
54 Stupefying thing
55 Favor doer's comment
56 It can be dangerous when leaked
57 Like some sunbathers

DOWN

1 Tree with large seedpods on its trunk
2 Like many older Americans' French or Spanish
3 Not given to lumbering
4 Jacob ___, South African president beginning in 2009
5 Member of the Ennead
6 Attic character
7 Movement from Cuba?
8 Brass tacks
9 Sock sound
10 Bad attribution
11 Aim
12 Where to find some nuts
13 "My heart bleeds for you," often
15 It's known for its start-ups
21 Proceed wearily
24 Unleash
25 "The Once and Future King" figure
26 Extremely
27 Albuterol alleviates it
29 Like some Beanie Babies
31 Sensible
32 Head
33 Groove on an arrow
34 Mailing to a label
35 Pie-baking giant
40 Antares or Proxima Centauri
42 Poet who wrote "Do I dare / Disturb the universe?"
43 Yes or no follower
44 Focus of stereochemistry
45 Roman Demeter
47 Neckline?
48 Union ___
49 Baby sound
51 Verano, across the Pyrenees
53 Yours, in Turin

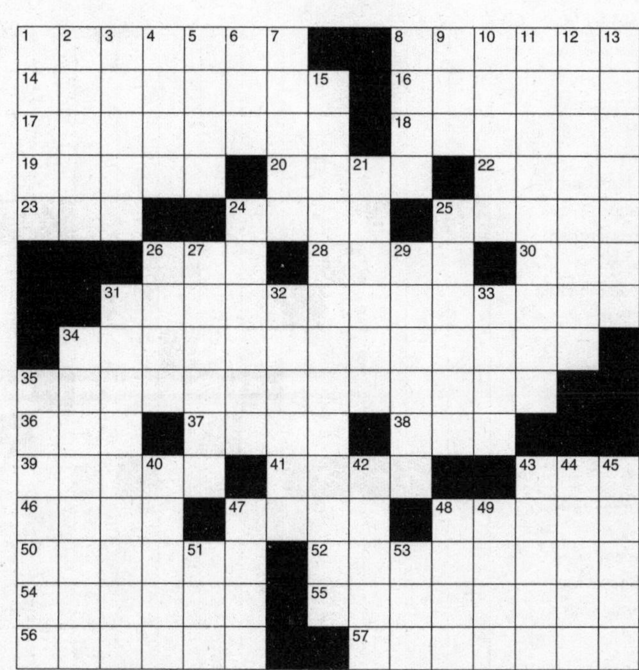

by Josh Knapp

60 HARD

ACROSS

1 What you may charge with
16 Indicator of how accurate a numerical guess is
17 Bringer of peace
18 The look of love?
19 One built for Broadway
20 Intel processor?
21 Pliers part
24 "The Chronicles of Clovis" author
26 Running dog
32 Opposite of extremely
34 Curing stuff, symbolically
36 Heffalump's creator
37 Title gambler in a 1943 Cary Grant film
39 Northern game preceder
41 Waits awhile
42 Eagles tight end Igwenagu
44 Make canning impossible?
45 Much commercial production
47 Flat
49 Some holiday honorees: Abbr.
50 Start of a Vol. 1 heading
52 Post-W.W. II fed. agcy.
54 Tone poem that calls for four taxi horns, with "An"
63 Past pump preference
64 Packing it in
65 Information information

DOWN

1 Some of them have learned to sign
2 Blowout locale?
3 "Thou ___ lady": King Lear
4 They might design roses
5 Visual aids
6 Like bazookas
7 1930s bomber
8 Not windy at all
9 Painter Schiele and composer Wellesz
10 Life is one
11 Their caps have a stylized "C"
12 Language related to Wyandot
13 Transporter of beer barrels
14 Captive of Heracles
15 Quarter of doce
21 Window parts
22 Like some anchors and sails
23 Not just another face in the crowd?
25 "The Inspector General" star, 1949
27 Org. that publishes Advocacy Update
28 Quarter of vingt
29 "Revolver" Grammy winner Voormann
30 Split up
31 "Deirdre" playwright
33 Certain recital piece
35 Kind of chop
38 Chi setting
40 One of several Procter & Gamble products
43 Chandra, in Hindu belief
46 Like a lot without a lot
48 Boot
51 Porsche 911 model
53 ___-foot jelly
54 Many masters respond to them
55 Cross
56 Hohenberg's river
57 Like line jumpers
58 First name in '70s tennis
59 Martin Buber's "___ Thou"
60 Shore indentations
61 Thomas H. ___, the Father of the Western
62 Calls on

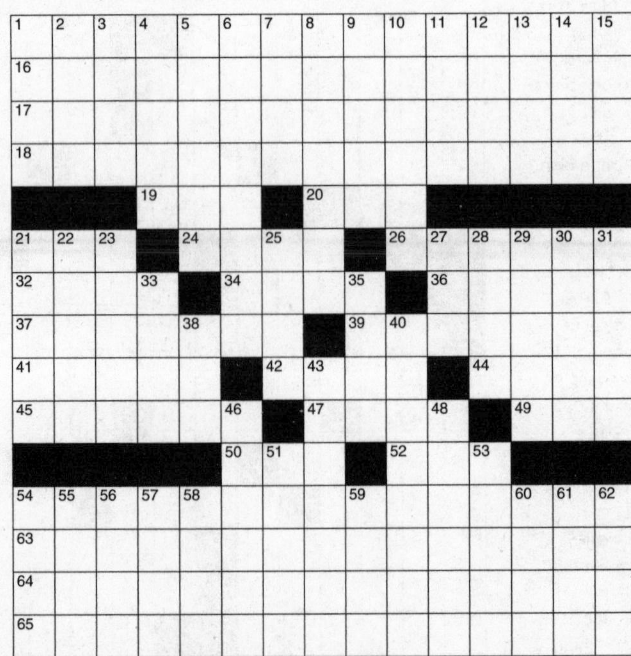

by Martin Ashwood-Smith

ACROSS

1 Comparable in extent
6 Old White House inits.
9 Convertible setting
14 Holdings
15 "Look at that!"
16 Laughing ___
17 Is curious about
20 N.Y.C. line
21 Some bulls
22 Stranded message?
23 Place to hang something
24 Off-putting?
28 Museum funding org.
29 Scale markings: Abbr.
30 Pajama-clad exec
31 It may help you get from E to F
37 Word with place or prayer
38 Stretch (out)
39 Besmirch
40 Long time
41 Bad quality for dangerous work
45 Put away
46 Google finding
47 Cool
48 Barely lost
54 H.S. subj.
55 Rocky mount
56 ___ o menos (basically, in Spanish)
57 Pooh pal
58 Drug study data
62 '90s soccer great Lalas
63 Prince Valiant's son
64 Onetime big name in daytime talk
65 Georges who wrote "Life: A User's Manual"
66 See 67-Across
67 With 66-Across, little source of carbs

DOWN

1 "___ of fools sailing on" (Wang Chung lyric)
2 1998's ___ Report
3 Notorious 1960s figure
4 Pension supplement, for short
5 Company of which Thomas Edison was once a director
6 Greets with a beep
7 One perhaps having one too many
8 Doctoral candidate's starting point
9 Large portion of Africa
10 Cries of despair
11 Source of hardwood?
12 18-Down, for one
13 Consumer products firm since 1837, informally
18 Dockworker's grp.
19 Infomercial pioneer Popeil
25 Fig. at the top of an organizational chart
26 Lao-___
27 Asian holiday
31 Big maker of S.U.V.'s
32 Moody's rating
33 Presidential nickname
34 It may be clicked on a computer
35 Cargo on the Spanish Main
36 Grandmother, to Brits
42 Fraternity letter
43 Start of a cheer
44 Japanese computer giant
48 Draw on again
49 Tropical lizard
50 Mauna ___
51 Mineo of movies
52 "I'm serious!"
53 Nurse, at times
59 Computer file suffix
60 ___-Magnon
61 Intl. broadcaster

by Joe Krozel

62 HARD

ACROSS

1 What's "all in my brain," in a 1967 rock classic
11 Dynasty founded by Yu the Great
15 Like some majors and wars
16 Capping
17 Be peerless
18 Blacks out
19 Little Joe's half brother of old TV
20 Einstein's death
21 Preakness, e.g.
22 Image mentale
24 First created being, in myth
26 Stand-up comic known for irreverent sermonettes
31 Form's top, perhaps
32 Make inseparable
33 River forming the Handegg waterfall
34 Having one 49-Across
35 Winner of seven tennis majors in the 1920s
38 Material in the translation process
39 Caterpillar roll ingredient
40 Operation creation
41 Java class?
43 Do a vanishing act
47 Jezebel's lack
48 One housed in a chest
49 See 34-Across
51 "Dear" one
52 Diamond stats
56 Decimal starter
57 Microsoft Office feature
60 Figure taking a bow?
61 No-strings declaration?
62 ___ deal
63 "So Wrong" singer, 1962

DOWN

1 Labor leader's cry?
2 It may precede itself
3 Stds. for A and E, e.g.
4 Seriously thinking
5 Monitor option, briefly
6 High
7 Headbands?
8 Longtime teammate of Mr. November
9 Eastern state?
10 City near Utrecht
11 Violent sandstorm
12 Old TV show hosted by Ed McMahon
13 Makeup of some beams
14 Basilica niche
21 Submitted
23 Product named for its "'round the clock protection"
24 Broccoli bits?
25 Foil component
26 Building with many sides
27 Fifth-century invader
28 ___-one
29 Stormed
30 Winner of 14 tennis majors in the 1990s
31 Wasn't straight
36 Many a college interviewer
37 Reference
42 Cylindrical menu item
44 What outer space is that cyberspace isn't?
45 Circular stack
46 Epsom's setting
49 Leave one's coat behind?
50 Saving type
51 Performer of high-risk operations
53 Mideastern P.M.'s nickname
54 Not blind to
55 Affliction whose name rhymes with its location
57 Vegas spot
58 German granny
59 American Crossroads, e.g.

by David Steinberg

ACROSS

1 "You doubt me?"
9 "Titus" director Taymor
14 Disappointing screen message
15 Series of movements
16 Start of a court display
17 Commensurate (with)
18 What we may be overseas?
19 Relative of a bathysphere
21 Limp Bizkit frontman Fred
23 Ingredient in some pastitsio
24 Sacha Baron Cohen character
25 Football stat.
26 21, in blackjack
28 Have words (with)
29 Earl of Sandwich, e.g.
30 What was once yours?
31 Some charge cards, informally
34 Wee
35 Florentine tourist attraction
36 Certainly didn't roar
39 Bellicose figure
40 Feature of a daredevil circus act
41 Dirt collector
44 Guinness measurement
45 Kool & the Gang's "Get Down ___"
46 Unsolicited manuscripts, informally
48 Get off the ground
51 Instruction for a violinist
52 It follows a curtain opening
53 Hood's support
55 Stir
56 Breather?
57 Gretzky, for most of the 1980s
58 Manages

DOWN

1 Big to-do, maybe?
2 Push to the limit
3 "That cuts me to the quick"
4 Houdini's real name
5 Take the money and run?
6 J. M. W. Turner's "___ Banished From Rome"
7 YouTuber, e.g.
8 It keeps people grounded
9 "Fear of Flying" author
10 Brazen
11 Accessory to a suit
12 Many early 20th-century U.S. immigrants
13 Blend with bergamot
15 ___-law
20 Gossip column subject
22 Not live
27 Function of mathematics: Abbr.
29 It's a living thing
30 Much of the Disney Channel's demographic
31 Gets comfortable with
32 Style played on a guitarrón
33 State of stability
34 Shout repeated at a basketball game
36 ___-pedi
37 Causes of head-scratching
38 Hush-hush
40 Farrell of "In Bruges"
41 Hushed sound
42 Get high
43 Strings along a beach?
47 1972 hit that begins "What'll you do when you get lonely . . . ?"
49 "___ leads to anger, anger leads to hate, hate leads to suffering": Yoda
50 "You have a point"
54 Naked

by Josh Knapp

64 HARD

ACROSS

1 Stephen King horror anthology
10 Yoke attachment
15 Great depression?
16 Egg choice
17 They're available in alleys
18 Wholly
19 Short play?
20 The King's followers?
21 Like some taxes and questions
22 Considered revolting
24 Struck
25 Pick
26 Home of the Aggies of the 37-Down
31 Below the surface
34 Québec map abbr.
35 Arena support?
36 Remove, as a 45-Across
38 Grand alternative
41 Trip option: Abbr.
42 She plagues ladies' lips with blisters, per Mercutio
44 Game of falling popularity?
45 It fits around a mouth
49 Bangladesh export
50 Using
51 Aviation safety statistic
55 What's often blowing in the wind
58 Show piece
59 Floral arrangement
60 Floor plan data
61 Painful spa treatment
63 Had an inclination
64 Nevertheless
65 Roman world
66 Justice from the Bronx

DOWN

1 What a speaker may strike
2 Nepalese bread
3 Classic Meccano toy
4 Midwest trailer?
5 Embedded column
6 Hardly any
7 Haydn's "master of us all"
8 Upstate New York natives
9 Unseld of the Bullets
10 Twist in fiction
11 Hit soundtrack album of 1980
12 Stationery securer
13 Look while delivering a line
14 Metalworker's union?
21 Leaving out
23 Grand
27 Good name for a brooder?
28 How many reach the top of Pikes Peak
29 Not grade-specific
30 Loses liquidity
31 Bellflower or Bell Gardens, vis-à-vis L.A.
32 Quaint preposition
33 Put down
37 New Mexico State sports grp.
39 "Cloth diaper" or "film camera"
40 Bullet follower
43 Frito ___ (old ad symbol)
46 Cable channel with the slogan "Laugh More"
47 Doesn't level with
48 Check out for a second
52 Certain building block, informally
53 Former defense grp.
54 Knick foe
55 One with hot dates, maybe
56 ___ Biscuit (1912 debut)
57 Spare
61 Low, in Lyon
62 Portfolio part, for short

by Barry C. Silk

ACROSS

1 Dupe
8 Like many PDFs
15 Red-hot
16 Letter
17 Salvage a bad situation
19 Hungarian city known for "Bull's Blood" wine
20 One catching the game
21 Two-time Best Rock Album Grammy winner
22 Acted like a sponge
24 Neighbor of Hercules
25 Critical hosp. setting
26 Founding member of the Star Alliance, for short
27 Automaker Adam
30 Mole removal option
32 Goth relative
33 "___ Bein' Bad" (Sawyer Brown country hit)
36 25-Across sights
37 Flipped out
40 Swinging halter, for short
41 Almost fall
42 Last item bagged, often: Abbr.
45 Milling byproducts
47 "___ Plays Monterey" (posthumous 1986 album)
48 Chairman ___ (hoops nickname)
49 1958–61 polit. alliance
50 Roger Staubach's sch.
53 Home of Sinbad the sailor
55 "Idol ___" (Mozart aria)
56 Cold war weapon?
59 Sorority letters
60 Too pooped to pop
63 Mathematical physicist Roger
64 Assorted
65 Have meals delivered
66 Like some tea

DOWN

1 Mature
2 Antes up for peanuts?
3 Open house invitation
4 Rear admiral's rear
5 Iguana, maybe
6 Music to a masseur's ears
7 Troglodytes troglodytes
8 Grinding material
9 Jack Benny persona
10 Like some giants and dwarfs
11 Prefix with kinetic
12 Why "there's no time for fussing and fighting," per a Beatles hit
13 Shows that one has
14 GPS button
18 Go for broke
23 Kind of beef
28 Fresh
29 Couch attachment?
31 2008 TARP recipient
34 Humanoid cryptid
35 Feel
38 Part of many a German name
39 Smidgen
40 It shows small parts of the picture
43 Whoop it up
44 Like many newlyweds and bagels
45 "Leatherstocking Tales" hero
46 One may give a ring
51 "My bad, Mario!"
52 Spiff (up), in dialect
54 See 62-Down
57 Some indicator lamps, briefly
58 "The Little Mermaid" prince
61 Post-hurricane handout, for short
62 With 54-Down, Best Supporting Actress nominee for 1945's "Mildred Pierce"

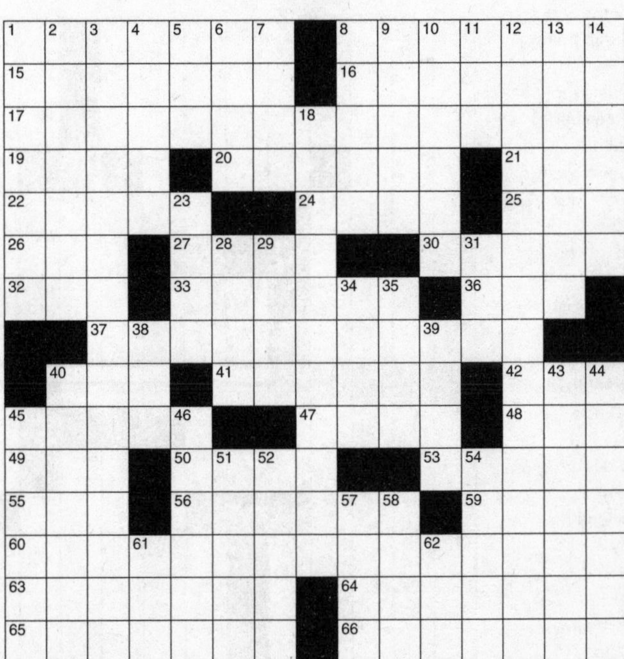

by Ed Sessa

66 HARD

ACROSS

1 One was first purchased in 2008
10 Big top features?
15 Title for Schwarzenegger
16 Half of a TV duo
17 One going through the exercises?
18 Leader of the Silver Bullet Band
19 Silence fillers
20 One might be apparent
21 See
22 Bit
24 "Toast of the Town" host
28 Grunt
29 1991 International Tennis Hall of Fame inductee
30 Cliff dweller
31 Ambulance supply
34 Game with points
35 Tired
36 Outfielder who was a member of baseball's All-Century Team
40 Digs, with "on"
42 ___ glass
43 1955 doo-wop hit
46 Peace Nobelist Cassin
47 Crooked bones?
51 Trix alternative?
52 Construction support
53 Drying device
55 2012 Seth MacFarlane comedy
56 Sound
58 Oath
60 Impala relative
61 Crisp salad ingredient from across the Pacific
62 Satisfy
63 Child support payer, in modern lingo

DOWN

1 "Can't wait!"
2 Opening
3 Item used in an exotic massage
4 Cheer with an accent
5 When doubled, a taunt
6 Host
7 Horticultural headache
8 Some landings
9 6 is a rare one
10 From overseas?
11 Lending figure
12 Northern Quebec's ___ Peninsula
13 Some Vatican art
14 Still
23 Athlete's booster
25 Ally
26 Race assignments
27 W.W. II inits.
31 Rose
32 Full of oneself
33 Roman numeral that's also a name
37 Like most sandals
38 Moneymaker topping a website
39 Milk and milk and milk
41 Common cocktail component
43 Common cocktail components
44 Cricket violation
45 Yellow Teletubby
48 2008 documentary about the national debt
49 Antilles native
50 Bacon product
54 Mind
57 W.W. II inits.
58 Meter site
59 New Deal program, for short

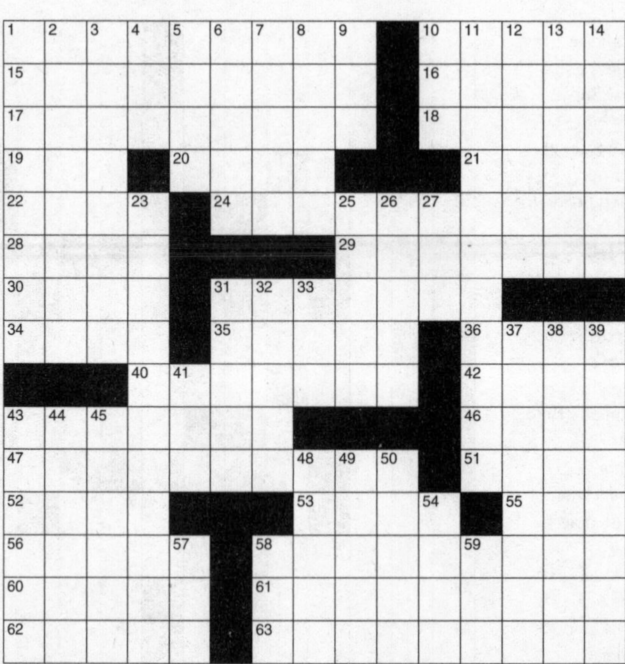

by David Quarfoot

ACROSS

1 Low interest indicator
5 Stick
9 "Debts and ___ are generally mixed together": Rabelais
13 Give a second hearing?
14 Go places
15 Buffet table utensil
16 His death prompted Georges Pompidou to say "France is a widow"
19 Show stopper
20 Church cry
21 Spoke lovingly
22 Vegas casino that hosts the World Series of Poker, with "the"
23 Celebrated race-horse nicknamed "The Red Terror"
25 Furniture usually with pillows
28 Hangs on
29 Surfing area?
31 Light weapon
32 Uppercut targets
33 Pier 1 furniture material
34 Not looking 100% well
35 Bad, for good
36 Singer Taylor
37 Notwithstanding
39 Soft lens's makeup
40 Jewelry chain
41 Ultimate problem solver
45 Words after "Oh well"
48 Loaded roll
49 They rate high on the Beaufort scale
50 Pot addition
51 Terminus of the old Virginia and Truckee Railroad
52 Ziploc competitor
53 They're often bagged
54 "This is quite a surprise!"

DOWN

1 Less polite way of saying "no thanks" to offered food
2 Evidence of an allergic reaction
3 Collides with noisily
4 1979 film based on the life of Crystal Lee Sutton
5 Pink fuel
6 Opera with the aria "Recondita armonia"
7 Volkswagen subsidiary
8 Getting through
9 Daphne, after her mythical transformation
10 Wasted, as time
11 "Phantom Lady" co-star Raines
12 Go for
15 Exerts oneself
17 Survivor of two 1918 assassination attempts
18 Rejoices tactlessly
23 "The American Crisis" pamphleteer
24 One of the Colonial Colleges, informally
25 Ground water?
26 Paperless way to read the paper
27 Only founding member of OPEC not located in the Mideast
28 "Come again?"
30 Wax worker
32 Ad agency acquisition
33 Fried appetizer
35 Flares
36 Summer Triangle star
38 Not to be disrespected
39 River mentioned in the Rig Veda
41 Historic caravel
42 Bar rooms?
43 Tennis's Dementieva
44 Many a filling material
45 One with a job opening?
46 Like the leaves of a trailing arbutus
47 Robert Louis Stevenson described it as "bottled poetry"

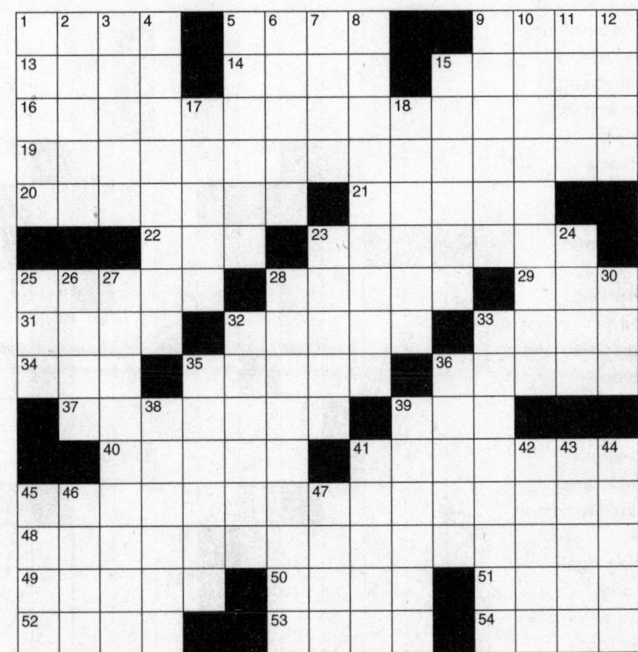

by Patrick Berry

68 HARD

ACROSS

1 Place to pick vegetables
9 With 25-Across, it has a huge trunk
15 C-worthy
16 Ancient abstainer
17 Buzzer sounded during a match
18 Small house of the Southwest
19 Whence Parmenides
20 Bubkes
22 See 23-Across
23 With 22-Across quits dragging
25 See 9-Across
27 Special recognition?
28 They result when solidly hit baseballs are caught
31 Royale maker
32 Major cleanups follow them
35 Starting catcher in every All-Star Game from 1964 to 1967
37 Name meaning "God is with us"
38 Go
40 Four French quarters?
41 They're likely to result in broken limbs
43 Claptrap
44 Prey for gray wolves
46 It has a Bridges and Tunnels div.
47 "Home away from home" sloganeer
48 "Until next time"
52 Vindictive Quaker of fiction
54 Like unabridged dictionaries
57 Angel, e.g., for short
58 Wonder Lake's national park
60 It stays the same
62 Site of a 1944 British Army defeat
63 Nourishing stuff
64 Treating badly
65 "S.N.L." segment

DOWN

1 Takes into account?
2 No longer in the minority
3 Bad thing to be breached
4 Water board
5 Old brand that promised "white white washes without red hands"
6 Guthrie's follower at Woodstock
7 Hun king, in myth
8 Frequent tour guide
9 Saxophone great Sidney
10 White sheet insert?
11 Fêmur, por exemplo
12 Goof
13 Herpetologist's supply
14 Six Gallery reading participants
21 Like some garlic and egos
24 "I goofed . . . big whoop"
26 Heir restoration targets?
29 Gas hog, briefly
30 Lock remover of old?
32 Formal opening
33 Answering machine notification
34 1836 siege leader
36 Sole mate?
39 Journal ender
42 Some Toyotas
45 Last month
49 Ethiopian grazer
50 Gossip girl
51 Like craft fairs
53 German way
55 Buzz on "The Simpsons," e.g.
56 Use a ball winder
59 Cry from some judges
61 Conference USA member, for short

by Ned White

ACROSS

1 Dinner spread
11 Streets of Rage maker
15 Gardening brand
16 Roman 18-Across
17 Former "Weekend Update" host on "S.N.L."
18 Greek 16-Across
19 Three-time All-Star pitcher Robb
20 Karnak Temple deity
22 Airport on Flushing Bay, in brief
23 "My Baby No ___ Aqui" (Garth Brooks song)
25 Family head
26 When the French celebrate Labor Day
27 Box fillers
30 Line to Wall Street, for short
31 N.B.A.'s Magic, on sports tickers
32 Responded to a dentist's request
33 Emblem
35 ___ failure
36 Critic Ebert, informally
37 Element with a low atomic number that is not found naturally on Earth
38 They cross many valleys
40 Gracefully quit
41 Time gap
42 Chris with the 1978 hit "Fool (If You Think It's Over)"
43 Antiquity
44 ___ glance
45 Its first complete ed. was published in 1928
46 Is worthwhile
47 0
48 Hot
50 T.A.'s pursuit, maybe
53 "Sure ___!"
55 Ruin the surprise, perhaps
58 Gadget's rank in cartoons: Abbr.
59 On- and off-road
60 Cruising
61 Movie mogul whom Forbes magazine once named the highest-paid man in entertainment

DOWN

1 Fed concerned with forgery
2 "Paris, Je T'___" (2006 film)
3 Leader in women's education?
4 Sitting formation
5 Prefix with sphere
6 Slip-preventing, in a way
7 ___ Brothers
8 View lasciviously
9 Hot
10 "Ye gods!"
11 Kind of request in a Robert Burns poem
12 N.B.A. Hall-of-Famer who, with Walt Frazier, formed the Knicks' "Rolls Royce Backcourt"
13 Outgoing
14 Hit makers, say
21 Bacterium binder
23 Old lab burners
24 Common sushi garnish
27 TV sketch comedy set in the "city where young people go to retire"
28 They're ordered by mathematicians
29 Some French-speaking Africans
33 Apple's mobile/tablet devices run on it
34 Red-carpet interview topics
36 Like some files
39 Views lasciviously
40 "Bigger & ___," 1999 Grammy-winning comedy album by Chris Rock
43 It's a downer
49 Giveaway
50 Jelly Belly flavor
51 Willing participant?
52 Fashion company with a Big Apple flagship store
54 Thermal ___
56 Calder contemporary
57 Historic beginning?

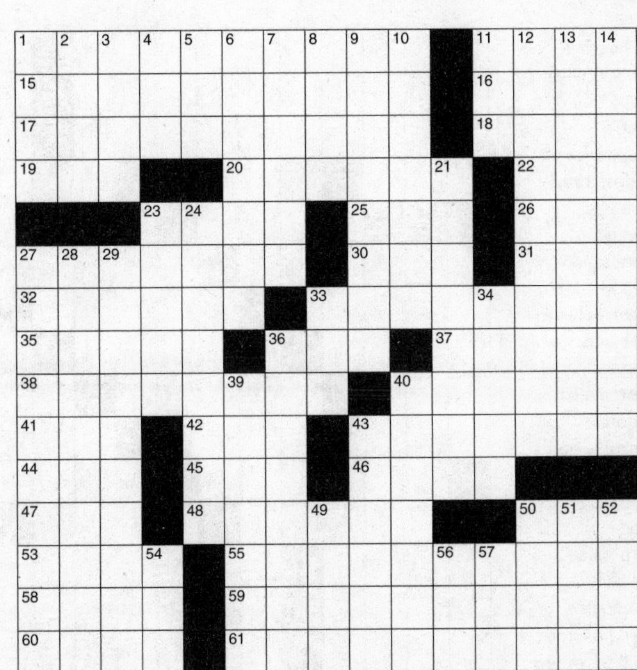

by Michael Sharp

70 HARD

ACROSS

1 Old easy-to-load shooter
11 Comparative follower
15 Pitching technique?
16 Government auction action
17 Toe-tapping trigger
18 Kissers
19 Some fridges
20 Dot in an atlas
21 How close-up magicians move
23 Home of some frogs
24 Fixed a broken web link?
25 Says "You said it!," say
28 Miss swinging at a piñata?
30 Thugs
31 Tiny bit
32 Taste test
33 Memo heads-up
34 Customer counter, maybe
35 Coloring
36 It airs episodes of "Episodes," briefly
37 François's following?
38 Keep the squeaking out of, say
39 It's drawn between similar things
41 Bantam
42 Teaching model
43 Small doses?
44 Green traffic sight?
45 Lift in greeting
46 City and state follower
49 Nero's position?
50 "A Tale of Two Cities" ender?
53 Some Fr. honorees
54 Where the Garden State Parkway meets I-280
55 Lake ___ (largest lake in Australia)
56 Stop on the way from 0 to 60?

DOWN

1 "Cool, bro"
2 Norton Sound port
3 Concessions
4 Skipping sound?
5 Outfits
6 Nephew of Matty and Jesus
7 She released "21" in 2011
8 It might be harsh or hushed
9 It oversees a major production every two yrs.
10 Plausibility
11 Strive to reach
12 One of Superman's powers
13 Cosmo alternatives
14 Busy
22 Battle of Endor combatant
23 Andrew Johnson's home: Abbr.
24 Rocks from socks
25 Audibly amazed
26 Penguin's habitat?
27 Line opener
28 Series of selling points
29 With relevance
31 Winter malady
34 Acts as if money were no object
35 Little props
37 Seltzer starter
38 He starred as Gatsby in 1974
40 Pin something on
41 Cookware cover
43 Very, to Verdi
44 Ovidian infinitive
45 Either side of an Oreo
46 Fan's pub
47 Young Frankenstein married her
48 Kind of review
51 Fujairah's locale: Abbr.
52 Hanger in a clothing shop

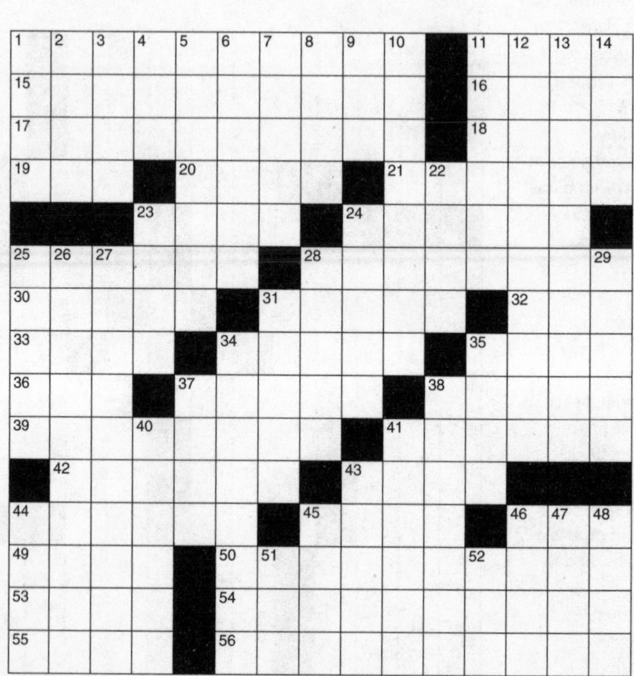

by Bruce R. Sutphin and Doug Peterson

HARD 71

ACROSS

1 Mobile home?
11 Made fun of, in a way
15 Bygone sportscaster with a statue outside Wrigley Field
16 Fan letters?
17 They may lead to another story
18 "Popular Fallacies" byline, 1826
19 Not so apple-cheeked
20 "Sure, I'm game"
22 Overzealous promgoer's choice, maybe
23 Address add-on
25 Noted press conference rhymer
26 What some swatches preview
27 Where Achilles was dipped to make him invincible
28 Representer of time, often
30 Part of a publicity agent's job
31 Ochoa who was the first #1-ranked golfer from Mexico
32 Waltz component
36 O, more formally
37 Fee on some out-of-state purchases
38 Bats
39 Longtime Capone rival
40 Lodging for a night out?
41 Single mom in a 2000s sitcom
45 Party to the Oslo Accords, for short
46 In the loop, with "in"
48 South Pacific palm
49 Business that may be a zoning target
51 Walk ostentatiously
52 Drop
53 Some contemporary ads
56 Chance upon
57 Unlikely pageant winners
58 Muddles
59 Many a John Wayne pic

DOWN

1 Scabbard
2 Base for Blackbeard
3 Fictional student at Riverdale High
4 Train track parts
5 Actors Talbot and Waggoner
6 Disney villain
7 Monopoly token
8 Spanish occupational suffix
9 Pitch producer
10 Dissolved, as bacteria exposed to antibodies
11 "Double" or "triple" move
12 Certain medieval combatant
13 Rhett Butler's "Frankly, my dear, I don't give a damn," e.g.
14 Nanny's order
21 State with Leipzig and Dresden
23 Stick in a cabinet
24 Objectivist Rand
27 X-ray ___
29 Chihuahua cry
30 Stop
31 What a brush may pick up
32 Ices
33 Common number of gondoliers
34 Intern's duty, maybe
35 Stop: Abbr.
36 Magician's prop
38 Lightning bolt shape
40 Mississippi site of Machine Gun Kelly's last known bank robbery
41 Close again, as a change purse
42 Emission of ripening fruit
43 Ending with flag or pall
44 Actress Milano of "Charmed"
47 Marked acidity
48 Earl Scruggs's instrument
50 The E.P.A. issues them: Abbr.
51 Cogent
54 Dial unit
55 "Encore!," to a diva

by Ian Livengood and Brad Wilber

72 HARD

ACROSS

1 Bloke
5 Proper partner?
9 Expressed out loud
11 Big name in folk music
13 Cubs cap display
15 Patroness of Québec
16 Defeat in a jump-rope competition, say
17 It's said to be the world's fastest field sport
18 More in need of a bath, say
19 Craigslist and others
20 Make sense
22 Rocker with the 1973 #1 hit "Frankenstein"
23 Spotted horse
24 Helpers for the deaf
30 Loitering
32 Arrangement of atoms in a crystal structure
33 Accounting department employees
35 Muscle that rotates a part outward
36 Definitely not a good looker?
37 "Standing room only"
38 Wash
39 Some jazz combos
40 Join up for another collaboration
41 Middling
42 Georgia and neighbors, once: Abbr.

DOWN

1 French hearts
2 Member of an ancient people known for warfare with chariots
3 Pretends to be sore
4 Christmas no-no
5 Views through a periscope, say
6 "It is through Art, and through Art only, that we can ___ our perfection": Oscar Wilde
7 Furnace part
8 Speed Stick brand
9 Certain YouTube posting
10 Little orange snacks
11 Sign over a car
12 Rules and ___
14 Some E.M.T. personnel
15 Living like husband and wife
21 Unpaid
24 Really would rather not
25 Menu heading
26 Hurriedly, in scores
27 Sedimentary rocks resembling cemented fish roe
28 Throats
29 Elvis Presley, notably
30 Post-hurricane scenes, e.g.
31 Fuel line additive
32 One side of a famous NBC feud
34 Look

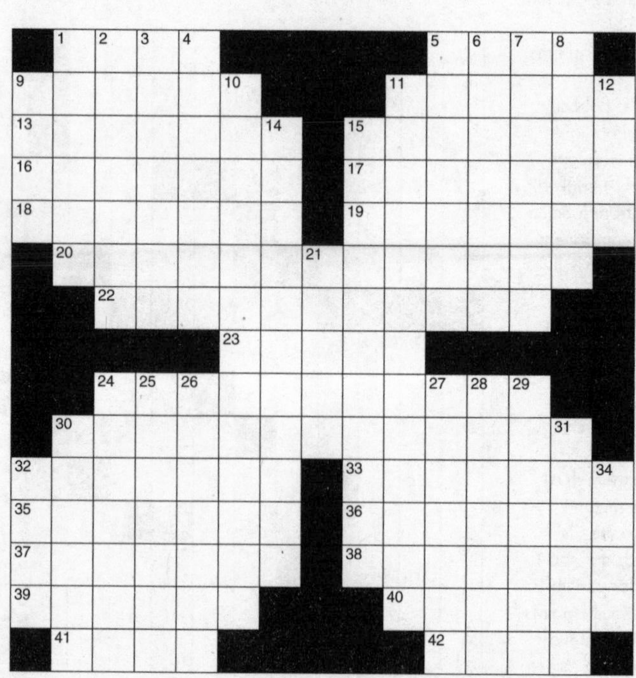

by Joe Krozel

ACROSS

1 Hall-of-Fame rock band or its lead musician
8 It sends out lots of streams
15 Very long European link
16 Rust or combust
17 It flies on demand
18 Skunk, at times
19 Some P.D. personnel
20 One who may be on your case
22 The Spanish I love?
23 What a couple of people can play
25 Stand-out performances
26 Chocolate bar with a long biscuit and caramel
27 Subject of the 2003 book "Power Failure"
29 Without hesitation
30 Subsist on field rations?
31 Its flowers are very short-lived
33 Like a sawhorse's legs
35 Critical
36 Party staple
37 Catered to Windows shoppers?
41 Noodle taxers?
45 Observes
46 Abbr. after 8-Across
48 Last band in the Rock and Roll Hall of Fame, alphabetically
49 "The Hudsucker Proxy" director, 1994
50 Columbia and the like
52 French river or department
53 "___ mentioned . . ."
54 Images on some lab slides
56 Lima-to-Bogotá dir.
57 Frankenstein, e.g.
59 Its passengers were revolting
61 Theodore Roosevelt Island setting
62 Destroyer destroyer
63 Colorful cooler
64 Makeover options

DOWN

1 Like some milk
2 Sashimi staple
3 Changing place
4 Blockbuster?
5 Mediums for dummies, say: Abbr.
6 Where it all comes together?
7 Ex amount?
8 Appointment disappointments
9 Nationals, at one time
10 Flag
11 Tablet banner, say, briefly
12 Reserve
13 Inventory
14 Duped
21 Gradual, in some product names
24 Giant in fantasy
26 Bar that's set very high
28 Physicist Bohr
30 Display on a red carpet
32 Basic solution
34 Without hesitation, in brief
37 Does some outdoor pitching?
38 "Don't joke about that yet"
39 Took away bit by bit
40 Event occasioning 7-Down
41 Cryotherapy choice
42 Artificially small
43 What might take up residence?
44 Truncated trunks?
47 Zero times, in Zwickau
50 Back-pedaler's words
51 About 7% of it is American
54 Vapor: Prefix
55 Apple assistant
58 Lib. arts major
60 Coral ___ (city near Oakland Pk., Fla.)

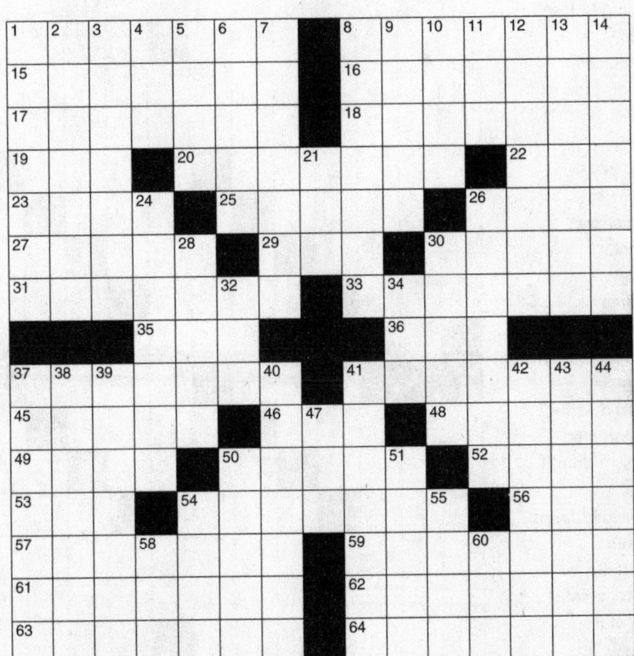

by Bruce R. Sutphin

74 HARD

ACROSS

1 It may provide closure in a tragedy
8 Discarded
15 City named for Theodore Roosevelt's vice president
17 Word search technique?
18 Webby Award winner who accepted saying "Please don't recount this vote"
19 With 11-Down, animal called "stubbin" by locals
20 Nascar stat that rises under caution flags
21 Diddly
22 Opening in the computer business?
23 Bad thing to lose
24 Flights
25 Taste makers?
26 Has it bad for, so to speak
27 -i relative
28 Largest city in Moravia
29 Mob member, informally
30 Morale
35 Second in command?
36 Cloverleaf section
37 Flat top
39 Blended dressing?
42 Shutter shutter
43 Literally, "I do not wish to"
44 Sauna exhalations
45 Solomonic
46 Chewed the fat
47 Watson's creator
48 Lowest of the low?
49 Prankery
50 1965 Beach Boys hit
53 Mission
54 Jason Mraz song that spent a record 76 weeks on Billboard's Hot 100
55 Outcries

DOWN

1 Outgoing
2 Lot arrangement
3 Draws
4 Some refrigerants
5 Reinforcement pieces
6 Mantel piece
7 Nissan bumpers?
8 Annual event since 1929, with "the"
9 Hard to pick up
10 Cigarette paper source
11 See 19-Across
12 Author of 1980's "The Annotated Gulliver's Travels"
13 Macedonia's capital
14 "El día que me quieras" and others
16 Large monitors
22 Abandon one's efforts, informally
23 "The Hound of the Baskervilles" backdrop
25 It's around a cup
26 1 Infinite ___ (address of Apple's headquarters)
28 Dover soul
29 Force in red uniforms: Abbr.
31 Course data
32 Palliate
33 Hit hard, as in an accident
34 Tip used for icing
38 They will be missed
39 Lightly hailed?
40 Major report
41 "Yowza!"
42 Hound
43 Dresden decimator of 1945
45 Something beyond the grate divide?
46 Herod's realm
48 1879's Anglo-___ War
49 "Fantastic Mr. Fox" author
51 War on Poverty agcy.
52 Advisory grp. that includes the drug czar

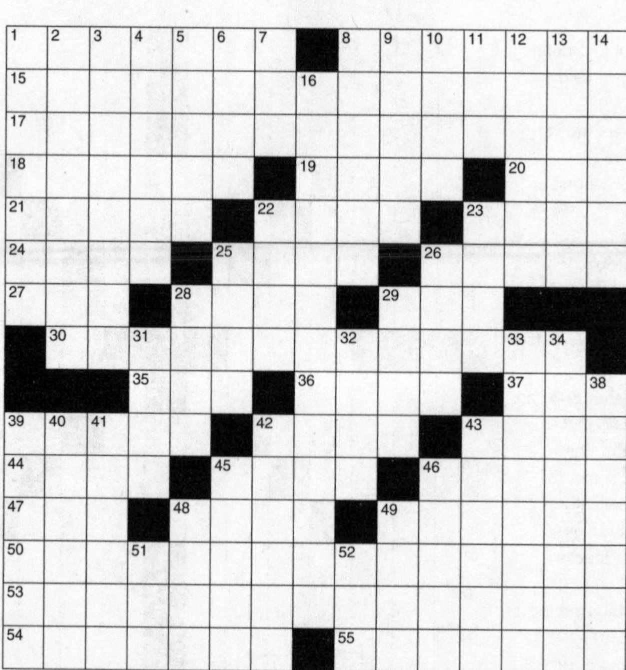

by Byron Walden

ACROSS

1 Forest newcomer
5 Group whose last Top 40 hit was "When All Is Said and Done"
9 To-do list
14 Sound after call waiting?
15 Sense, as a 14-Across
16 Nobel winner Joliot-Curie
17 Turkey sticker
20 "Everybody Is ___" (1970 hit)
21 Response to a threat
22 Old co. with overlapping globes in its logo
23 1960s civil rights leader ___ Brown
25 Katey who portrayed TV's Peg Bundy
27 Benchwarmer's plea
33 Drain
34 Bobby's follower?
35 Fibonacci, notably
36 Hockey Hall of Fame nickname
38 Alternative to ZzzQuil
40 Stat. for Re, La or Ti
41 "___ needed"
43 Papa ___ (Northeast pizza chain)
45 Now in
46 "That subject's off the table!"
49 Luster
50 They have edible shells
51 Whse. sight
53 "Philosophy will clip an angel's wings" writer
56 French class setting
59 Universal query?
62 Uncle Sam, say
63 One featuring a Maltese cross
64 Turkic word for "island"
65 Browser history list
66 Couldn't discard in crazy eights, say
67 Court suspensions

DOWN

1 Relief provider, for short
2 Blasts through
3 "And now?"
4 Sealing worker
5 "Per-r-rfect!"
6 ___-red
7 Alfred H. ___ Jr., founding director of MoMA
8 Like G.I.'s, per recruiting ads
9 Interval
10 Were present?
11 Gets payback
12 Sensed
13 They may be used in veins
18 They may be used around veins
19 All-Star Infante
24 Drone
26 1998 hit from the album "Surfacing"
27 False start?
28 Stockholders?
29 Like some hemoglobin
30 ___-A
31 Plantation habitation
32 Cybermemo
37 Something taken on the stand
39 Ring
42 They're on hunts
44 Revolving feature
47 Revolving features?
48 "Psst . . . buddy"
51 1/20 tons: Abbr.
52 Whence the word "bong"
54 Day of the week of Jul. 4, 1776
55 Wizened up
57 Indiana, e.g., to Lafayette
58 Some use electric organs
60 River Shannon's Lough ___
61 Sudoku segment

by Peter A. Collins

Smart Puzzles

Presented with Style

Available at your local bookstore or online at www.nytimes.com/nytstore

1

H	I	D	■	A	G	E	G	A	P	■	O	H	M	E
A	M	O	■	R	O	C	O	C	O	■	M	I	C	A
W	H	E	R	E	O	H	W	H	E	R	E	H	A	S
K	O	R	E	A	■	O	N	O	■	A	G	O	N	Y
■	■	■	G	M	C	■	S	O	N	I	A	■	■	■
■	R	E	G	A	L	E	■	■	I	N	S	P	O	T
O	E	D	I	P	U	S	R	E	X	■	■	E	W	E
R	A	G	E	S	■	T	A	G	■	P	L	E	N	A
E	T	E	■	■	R	A	N	G	E	R	O	V	E	R
M	A	D	M	A	X	■	■	S	E	E	P	E	D	■
■	■	■	E	L	S	I	E	■	C	S	I	■	■	■
A	L	E	R	O	■	D	V	R	■	A	N	D	U	P
M	Y	L	I	T	T	L	E	D	O	G	G	O	N	E
F	R	A	T	■	A	E	R	A	T	E	■	O	T	S
M	E	L	S	■	T	R	Y	S	T	S	■	M	O	O

2

A	S	T	R	A	■	E	I	D	E	R	■	C	A	B
L	I	R	A	S	■	L	D	O	P	A	■	O	V	I
A	G	A	S	P	■	F	I	R	E	P	O	W	E	R
W	H	I	T	E	S	M	O	K	E	■	P	E	R	T
■	S	T	A	R	E	A	T	■	■	B	E	R	T	H
■	■	■	■	S	T	N	■	O	D	I	N	■	■	■
S	P	I	C	E	S	■	B	I	R	D	B	A	T	H
E	A	C	H	■	H	O	U	S	E	■	A	L	S	O
C	L	E	A	N	O	U	T	■	A	I	R	B	A	G
■	■	■	N	O	T	I	■	P	M	S	■	■	■	■
A	C	I	N	G	■	■	T	R	O	O	P	E	R	■
W	A	N	E	■	G	R	E	E	N	L	I	G	H	T
F	U	L	L	C	O	U	R	T	■	A	E	R	I	E
U	S	A	■	A	G	E	N	T	■	T	R	E	N	D
L	E	W	■	M	O	S	S	Y	■	E	S	T	E	S

3

O	A	K	■	B	R	A	■	■	S	C	O	F	F	S
B	E	I	■	M	A	X	I	■	C	O	L	L	I	E
G	I	N	■	W	I	L	T	■	I	N	D	E	N	T
Y	O	G	I	■	D	E	S	K	■	S	E	X	E	S
N	U	A	N	C	E	■	R	A	N	T	S	■	■	■
■	■	R	U	H	R	■	A	L	C	A	T	R	A	Z
L	O	T	S	A	■	N	I	K	O	N	■	I	R	E
U	S	H	E	R	■	A	N	A	■	T	A	C	O	S
M	S	U	■	L	O	G	I	N	■	I	S	H	O	T
P	A	R	M	E	S	A	N	■	I	N	C	A	■	■
■	■	■	A	M	O	N	G	■	D	E	A	R	M	E
M	A	Z	D	A	■	O	M	N	I	■	P	D	A	S
S	M	U	D	G	E	■	E	C	O	N	■	I	N	T
R	E	L	E	N	T	■	N	A	T	O	■	I	D	O
P	R	U	N	E	S	■	■	A	S	S	■	I	M	P

4

G	S	A	■	O	P	E	R	A	■	A	N	A	I	S
O	W	L	■	M	O	P	U	P	■	H	E	N	R	I
W	I	L	D	G	E	E	S	E	■	H	A	T	E	D
E	T	U	I	■	S	E	E	M	■	■	R	I	F	E
S	C	R	E	W	Y	■	■	A	R	P	■	N	U	B
T	H	E	T	A	■	W	I	N	E	H	O	U	S	E
■	■	■	■	R	A	I	N	■	P	A	C	K	E	T
■	■	W	I	N	G	E	D	H	O	R	S	E	■	■
T	A	I	P	E	I	■	U	R	S	A	■	■	■	■
W	I	N	O	R	L	O	S	E	■	O	B	I	T	S
E	R	N	■	S	E	N	■	■	S	H	U	M	A	I
E	L	I	S	■	■	E	R	I	N	■	R	B	I	S
Z	I	P	U	P	■	W	I	S	E	C	R	A	C	K
E	N	E	R	O	■	A	T	B	A	T	■	C	H	E
S	E	G	E	R	■	Y	A	N	K	S	■	K	I	L

5

S	T	E	P	■	Y	A	M	S	■	A	D	Z	E	S
C	A	F	E	■	U	N	I	T	■	W	R	I	S	T
I	D	O	L	■	M	E	M	E	■	M	O	T	T	O
■	A	R	O	O	M	W	I	T	H	A	V	I	E	W
■	■	E	S	P	Y	■	■	■	O	N	E	■	■	■
M	A	F	I	A	■	A	G	R	O	■	M	O	L	D
A	T	F	■	R	E	R	E	A	D	■	A	H	O	Y
I	W	O	N	T	L	E	T	Y	O	U	D	O	W	N
D	A	R	E	■	L	A	G	O	O	N	■	L	E	E
S	R	T	A	■	I	R	O	N	■	A	B	Y	S	S
■	■	■	T	S	O	■	■	■	S	P	A	N	■	■
U	C	A	N	T	T	O	U	C	H	T	H	I	S	■
S	O	F	I	A	■	S	T	A	R	■	A	G	H	A
P	A	R	K	S	■	L	A	M	E	■	I	H	O	P
S	L	O	S	H	■	O	H	O	K	■	S	T	O	P

6

H	A	R	P	Y	■	T	H	U	S	■	T	H	E	M
O	H	A	R	A	■	H	O	S	T	■	H	O	B	O
W	A	T	E	R	W	A	T	E	R	■	E	M	A	J
■	S	A	Y	N	O	■	B	R	A	■	Y	O	Y	O
■	■	■	■	S	O	S	A	■	P	E	R	P	■	■
A	R	T	S	■	L	I	T	H	■	N	E	H	R	U
M	A	Y	O	■	E	X	H	O	R	T	■	O	H	S
A	N	C	I	E	N	T	■	M	A	R	I	N	E	R
S	C	H	■	A	S	H	C	A	N	■	R	E	T	D
S	H	O	P	S	■	S	A	G	A	■	E	S	T	A
■	■	B	A	T	S	■	L	E	W	D	■	■	■	■
P	E	R	T	■	E	A	T	■	A	R	U	B	A	■
A	M	A	H	■	E	V	E	R	Y	W	H	E	R	E
I	M	H	O	■	M	E	C	H	■	H	U	R	O	N
D	Y	E	S	■	E	C	H	O	■	O	H	G	O	D

7

R	O	B	E	■	F	E	R	N	■	M	I	C	A	H
A	P	E	X	■	A	L	I	A	■	C	R	A	N	E
H	I	G	H	■	R	O	T	T	E	N	E	G	G	S
M	E	S	A	A	R	I	Z	O	N	A	■	E	R	S
■	■	■	U	M	A	■	■	■	T	I	E	D	Y	E
A	M	E	S	B	R	O	T	H	E	R	S	■	■	■
M	U	L	T	I	■	B	O	O	R	■	P	E	R	P
P	C	B	■	T	R	E	N	T	O	N	■	Z	O	O
S	H	A	M	■	O	S	T	E	■	A	S	I	A	N
■	■	■	S	A	M	E	O	L	D	S	T	O	R	Y
T	O	P	G	U	N	■	■	■	E	A	U	■	■	■
A	R	E	■	S	E	A	M	W	E	L	D	I	N	G
B	E	A	U	T	Y	S	H	O	P	■	I	R	O	N
L	O	C	K	E	■	T	O	M	E	■	O	O	N	A
A	S	H	E	N	■	I	S	B	N	■	S	C	O	W

8

C	A	S	I	N	O	S	■	L	E	B	A	N	O	N
T	H	E	W	A	V	E	■	O	R	I	G	A	M	I
R	I	P	O	P	E	N	■	B	A	S	E	M	E	N
■	■	■	N	O	R	■	N	O	S	E	■	E	G	O
M	A	N	T	L	E	■	A	S	E	C	■	D	A	S
I	C	E	■	E	A	R	N	■	S	T	A	R	■	■
L	E	I	■	O	T	I	C	■	■	■	L	O	S	S
E	L	L	E	N	■	O	Y	L	■	D	E	P	T	H
R	A	D	S	■	■	■	D	E	N	Y	■	P	A	R
■	■	I	S	B	N	■	R	O	A	N	■	E	V	E
C	S	A	■	R	I	C	E	■	T	A	R	R	E	D
Y	A	M	■	A	C	O	W	■	U	M	A	■	■	■
S	N	O	O	Z	E	D	■	A	R	I	Z	O	N	A
T	A	N	L	I	N	E	■	L	A	T	E	R	A	L
S	A	D	D	L	E	S	■	P	L	E	D	G	E	S

9

L	C	D	■	M	C	G	R	U	F	F	■	E	S	C
I	O	U	■	A	E	R	O	S	O	L	■	T	A	L
M	M	M	■	G	R	A	N	D	B	A	H	A	M	A
B	A	B	Y	M	A	M	A	■	■	■	E	L	I	S
■	■	D	O	A	■	M	L	K	■	A	R	I	A	S
F	R	O	G	■	R	A	D	I	O	D	R	A	M	A
D	O	R	I	T	O	■	■	D	U	D	■	■	■	■
A	T	A	C	A	M	A	■	D	I	O	R	A	M	A
■	■	■	■	P	E	P	■	■	D	N	A	L	A	B
M	A	L	I	A	O	B	A	M	A	■	V	A	T	S
A	Y	E	R	S	■	S	P	A	■	S	E	N	■	■
R	E	N	O	■	■	■	O	N	E	L	L	A	M	A
V	A	S	C	O	D	A	G	A	M	A	■	L	A	N
E	Y	E	■	P	I	N	E	N	U	T	■	D	A	N
L	E	S	■	T	O	O	E	A	S	Y	■	A	M	A

10

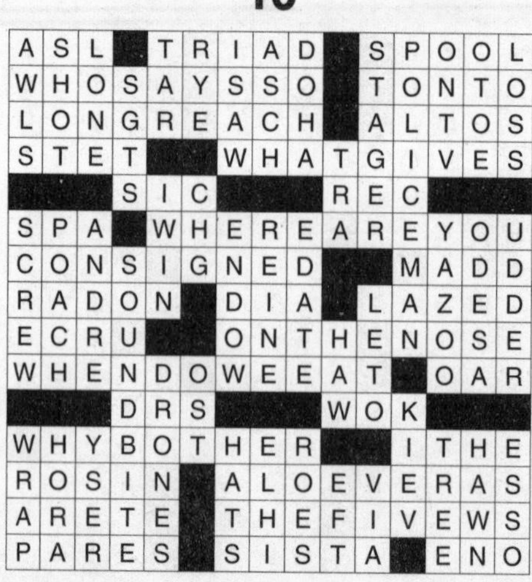

A	S	L	■	T	R	I	A	D	■	S	P	O	O	L
W	H	O	S	A	Y	S	S	O	■	T	O	N	T	O
L	O	N	G	R	E	A	C	H	■	A	L	T	O	S
S	T	E	T	■	■	W	H	A	T	G	I	V	E	S
■	■	■	S	I	C	■	■	■	R	E	C	■	■	■
S	P	A	■	W	H	E	R	E	A	R	E	Y	O	U
C	O	N	S	I	G	N	E	D	■	■	M	A	D	D
R	A	D	O	N	■	D	I	A	■	L	A	Z	E	D
E	C	R	U	■	■	O	N	T	H	E	N	O	S	E
W	H	E	N	D	O	W	E	E	A	T	■	O	A	R
■	■	■	D	R	S	■	■	■	W	O	K	■	■	■
W	H	Y	B	O	T	H	E	R	■	■	I	T	H	E
R	O	S	I	N	■	A	L	O	E	V	E	R	A	S
A	R	E	T	E	■	T	H	E	F	I	V	E	W	S
P	A	R	E	S	■	S	I	S	T	A	■	E	N	O

11

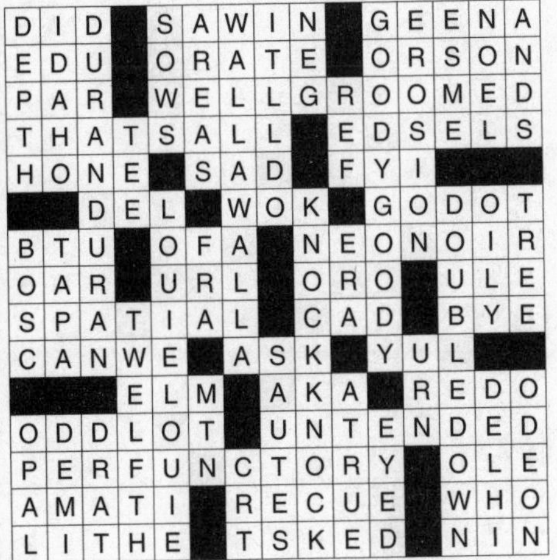

12

M	A	O	R	I		S	K	I	L		E	S	T	S
A	R	R	I	D		E	I	N	E		Z	O	O	T
S	P	A	C	E	B	A	R	G	E		R	O	P	E
		C	H	A	R	L	I	E	C	H	A	N	G	E
B	R	U	I	S	E			S	H	E		Y	U	L
R	O	L	E		W	H	E	T		P	L	I	N	Y
A	B	A		T	S	A	R		I	C	E			
	B	R	E	A	K	I	N	G	B	A	D	G	E	
			W	I	I		S	A	L	T		A	D	D
A	Z	T	E	C		S	T	Y	E		E	R	G	O
D	U	H		H	I	E			W	A	N	D	E	R
O	R	I	G	I	N	A	L	S	I	N	G	E		
R	I	C	O		E	V	I	L	T	W	I	N	G	E
E	C	K	O		P	E	S	O		A	N	I	M	A
S	H	E	D		T	R	A	P		R	E	A	C	T

13

C	E	D	A	R		Z	I	O	N		P	H	I	L
A	M	O	R	E		I	R	A	E		R	O	N	A
P	I	G	I	N	A	P	O	K	E		E	G	G	Y
E	L	I	E		E	O	N		D	A	S	H	E	S
S	E	E	T	H	R	U		O	S	O	L	E		
			T	O	O	T	A	T		K	E	A	N	U
J	I	H	A	D	S		T	O	W		Y	V	E	S
U	S	A		S	O	W	S	E	A	R		E	R	E
D	E	M	I		L	I	E		S	O	U	N	D	S
D	E	F	O	E		C	A	R	H	O	P			
		I	N	I	N	K		A	T	T	A	C	H	E
A	S	S	I	S	I		G	N	U		T	A	I	L
R	I	T	Z		P	O	R	K	B	A	R	R	E	L
A	L	E	E		A	R	A	L		D	E	E	R	E
B	O	D	S		T	O	B	E		S	E	W	O	N

14

C	M	D	R		R	O	B	O	T		M	P	E	G
R	O	U	E		E	D	I	T	H		I	A	M	A
A	R	B	S		A	D	D	T	O		N	U	M	B
B	R	A	E	S		B	E	E		I	S	L	A	S
S	A	I	N	T	P	A	T	R	I	C	K			
			T	U	L	L		S	R	O		F	D	A
S	C	A	F	F	O	L	D		E	N	U	R	E	S
O	A	H	U			S	E	A			N	A	S	H
I	M	E	L	D	A		I	R	O	N	D	U	K	E
R	E	M		R	H	O		M	O	L	E			
			S	N	A	K	E	C	H	A	R	M	E	R
C	I	N	C	O		A	N	A		T	W	I	N	E
A	M	A	H		L	Y	N	N	E		E	D	D	Y
P	A	T	E		S	E	E	D	S		A	G	U	E
E	Y	E	D		D	D	A	Y	S		R	E	P	S

15

N	I	C	E			A	R	T	Y		C	R	T	S
I	M	U	S		L	O	E	W	E		L	O	I	N
P	A	T	P	A	U	L	S	E	N		A	U	T	O
P	G	S		S	N	E	E	R		C	I	G	A	R
Y	E	S		P	A	R	T	P	A	Y	M	E	N	T
		H	I	S					C	B	S			
A	M	O	R		C	R	E	A	T	E		L	O	P
P	A	R	A	L	L	E	L	P	A	R	K	I	N	G
T	O	T		L	A	D	I	E	S		I	K	E	A
			E	A	R					G	T	E		
P	A	J	A	M	A	P	A	R	T	Y		I	P	O
O	P	E	R	A		A	D	L	E	R		C	U	B
I	N	S	T		C	O	M	E	T	O	P	A	P	A
S	E	T	H		E	L	I	S	E		T	R	I	M
E	A	S	Y		L	O	T	S			S	E	L	A

16

A	C	C	T	■	E	C	H	O	■	L	A	P	I	S
N	O	L	A	■	L	R	O	N	■	E	V	E	N	T
D	R	U	G	A	B	U	S	E	■	T	E	R	S	E
R	E	N	A	M	E	■	E	D	A	M	■	D	I	E
E	A	G	L	E	■	L	A	G	B	E	H	I	N	D
■	■	■	O	B	I	E	■	E	R	G	O	T	■	■
P	U	B	G	A	M	E	S	■	I	O	N	I	Z	E
E	V	A	■	■	S	K	I	E	D	■	■	O	E	D
W	A	R	M	T	O	■	B	I	G	B	A	N	D	S
■	■	B	L	U	R	B	■	N	E	A	T	■	■	■
C	R	A	B	G	R	A	S	S	■	A	T	A	R	I
Y	E	R	■	B	Y	T	E	■	Z	E	A	L	O	T
C	A	I	R	O	■	M	I	X	E	D	B	A	G	S
L	I	A	N	A	■	A	K	I	N	■	O	N	E	O
E	R	N	S	T	■	N	O	N	O	■	Y	A	R	N

17

T	O	A	S	T	■	H	A	R	A	■	F	A	D	S
I	R	A	Q	I	■	Y	V	E	S	■	I	C	E	T
V	I	R	U	S	■	D	I	S	C	■	R	I	P	A
O	G	E	E	■	P	R	A	I	R	I	E	D	O	G
■	■	■	A	R	E	A	■	D	I	G	E	S	T	S
J	A	C	K	I	N	T	H	E	B	O	X	■	■	■
O	R	O	■	O	N	E	A	■	E	R	I	C	A	S
B	L	O	C	■	■	S	R	A	■	■	T	A	M	E
S	O	L	O	N	G	■	P	V	T	S	■	L	O	W
■	■	■	C	A	R	D	O	O	R	L	O	C	K	S
K	O	O	K	I	E	R	■	C	O	O	T	■	■	■
I	N	T	E	R	N	E	T	A	D	■	E	G	O	S
T	R	E	Y	■	A	W	E	D	■	S	L	O	A	N
E	Y	R	E	■	D	O	N	O	■	A	L	O	H	A
R	E	I	D	■	E	N	D	S	■	P	O	P	U	P

18

A	B	B	R	■	S	T	A	R	C	H	■	Q	E	D
S	E	R	A	■	E	R	I	E	P	A	■	E	A	U
T	H	A	W	■	R	O	D	E	O	D	R	I	V	E
R	A	Y	D	A	V	I	E	S	■	■	H	I	E	S
O	N	S	A	L	E	■	■	E	L	L	Y	■	■	■
■	■	■	T	O	S	I	R	■	A	T	M	F	E	E
A	F	L	A	T	■	R	A	I	N	D	E	L	A	Y
T	W	O	■	■	R	A	N	D	D	■	■	E	R	R
R	I	N	G	D	A	N	C	E	■	G	R	A	P	E
A	W	G	E	E	Z	■	H	A	I	L	E	■	■	■
■	■	■	N	A	R	C	■	■	M	A	D	C	A	P
C	H	A	I	■	■	R	O	A	L	D	D	A	H	L
R	I	V	E	R	D	E	L	T	A	■	A	M	M	O
U	F	O	■	V	I	D	I	O	T	■	W	E	E	P
Z	I	N	■	S	N	O	O	Z	E	■	N	O	D	S

19

E	S	S	E	■	B	L	O	B	■	■	B	A	C	H
G	L	E	E	■	B	O	N	E	■	P	A	U	L	A
G	I	R	L	S	C	O	U	T	■	A	S	T	I	R
S	M	A	S	H	■	■	S	T	A	N	H	O	P	E
■	■	■	■	A	L	I	■	O	B	I	■	■	■	■
■	G	R	A	H	A	M	C	R	A	C	K	E	R	S
D	I	E	T	■	P	A	L	■	■	S	A	R	E	E
I	S	L	E	■	S	M	O	R	E	■	B	A	N	E
S	M	E	A	R	■	■	T	O	G	■	U	T	E	P
H	O	T	M	A	R	S	H	M	A	L	L	O	W	■
■	■	■	■	T	U	T	■	A	D	O	■	■	■	■
C	H	E	S	T	N	U	T	■	■	C	E	D	A	R
A	U	R	A	L	■	C	H	O	C	O	L	A	T	E
M	E	R	L	E	■	C	R	A	B	■	S	H	O	P
P	S	S	T	■	■	O	U	R	S	■	E	L	M	S

20

G	O	P	R	O	■	B	A	R	■	S	K	I	C	A	P
I	N	F	E	R	■	O	R	E	■	P	E	L	O	S	I
F	A	C	E	B	O	O	K	S	T	A	L	K	I	N	G
■	■	■	L	I	D	■	■	C	A	R	■	■	N	E	G
■	B	E	S	T	D	O	C	U	M	E	N	T	A	R	Y
C	A	D	I	Z	■	G	R	E	■	R	A	M	P	■	■
O	M	E	N	■	T	R	I	P	■	I	T	Z	H	A	K
I	B	N	■	T	H	E	M	A	M	B	O	■	R	U	N
T	I	P	T	O	E	■	E	R	O	S	■	I	A	G	O
■	■	R	A	R	A	■	W	T	O	■	I	N	S	E	T
I	M	A	G	I	N	A	R	Y	N	U	M	B	E	R	■
T	O	I	■	■	S	R	I	■	■	A	F	R	■	■	■
W	O	R	D	S	W	I	T	H	F	R	I	E	N	D	S
A	R	I	O	S	E	■	E	A	R	■	N	E	A	R	S
S	E	E	G	E	R	■	R	H	O	■	E	D	G	E	R

21

V	O	L	S	■	C	O	P	T	O	■	S	L	A	V
A	V	O	W	■	I	N	L	A	W	■	H	I	V	E
N	A	V	I	■	G	E	E	S	E	■	A	V	E	S
E	L	E	V	E	■	A	B	E	■	E	V	I	C	T
■	■	R	E	V	E	L	■	R	A	V	E	N	■	■
K	I	S	L	E	V	■	■	■	V	I	R	G	I	N
O	W	L	■	R	E	V	I	V	A	L	■	W	H	O
L	O	A	D	■	N	I	V	E	N	■	L	I	O	N
A	N	N	E	■	S	C	A	N	T	■	A	L	P	O
S	T	E	E	L	■	A	N	E	■	M	I	L	E	S
■	■	■	M	I	G	R	A	T	I	O	N	■	■	■
S	P	A	■	M	O	I	■	I	N	N	■	B	A	D
T	O	R	P	E	D	O	■	A	N	I	M	A	T	E
U	P	T	O	Y	O	U	■	N	I	C	E	J	O	B
D	E	S	I	S	T	S	■	S	E	A	L	A	N	T

22

■	T	A	M	P	■	S	W	A	P	■	R	A	S	P
S	A	R	A	H	■	T	O	D	O	■	U	T	A	H
T	H	E	R	E	G	O	E	S	M	Y	B	A	B	Y
D	O	W	■	W	I	K	I	■	■	A	I	D	E	S
S	E	E	N	■	D	E	S	S	E	R	T	■	■	■
■	■	A	F	T	E	R	M	I	D	N	I	G	H	T
D	O	L	L	S	■	■	E	S	E	■	N	E	A	R
R	H	O	■	A	B	S	■	I	N	C	■	T	R	A
E	O	N	S	■	A	A	S	■	■	B	A	T	T	Y
W	H	E	E	L	I	N	T	H	E	S	K	Y	■	■
■	■	■	N	O	T	E	P	A	D	■	A	S	A	P
T	W	E	E	N	■	■	E	R	G	O	■	B	R	A
S	I	N	G	I	N	G	T	H	E	B	L	U	E	S
A	N	N	A	■	A	S	E	A	■	E	A	R	N	S
R	E	E	L	■	B	A	R	R	■	Y	O	G	A	■

23

C	H	O	O	■	■	E	T	H	I	C	■	D	O	S
H	A	S	H	■	L	A	R	E	D	O	■	R	N	A
A	R	T	I	■	A	T	A	R	I	S	■	E	L	Y
■	■	L	O	S	T	■	P	R	O	M	I	S	E	S
B	R	E	A	K	E	R	■	■	M	O	N	D	A	Y
L	O	R	N	A	■	E	P	I	■	S	T	E	V	E
T	D	S	■	T	B	T	E	S	T	■	O	N	E	S
■	■	■	L	E	T	I	T	S	N	O	W	■	■	■
A	T	T	A	■	W	E	E	U	N	S	■	R	C	A
T	H	R	U	M	■	D	R	E	■	A	S	I	A	N
H	E	A	R	Y	E	■	■	S	A	M	E	O	L	D
L	O	C	A	T	I	O	N	■	G	A	L	L	■	■
E	M	I	■	H	E	L	E	N	A	■	D	O	T	H
T	E	N	■	O	I	L	C	A	R	■	O	B	I	E
E	N	G	■	S	O	A	K	S	■	■	M	O	N	Y

24

T	A	P	E	■	G	A	P	E	■	■	N	A	L	A
N	E	I	N	■	A	L	O	T	■	M	O	T	O	R
U	S	A	I	N	B	O	L	T	■	A	T	T	I	C
T	O	N	G	A	■	U	S	U	A	L	F	A	R	E
■	P	O	M	P	S	■	■	■	B	L	A	R	E	D
■	■	B	A	S	I	N	■	S	A	R	I	■	■	■
S	E	A	S	■	B	O	S	C	■	A	R	T	S	Y
P	A	R	■	U	S	B	P	O	R	T	■	A	T	E
A	R	S	O	N	■	L	Y	L	E	■	U	L	E	E
■	■	■	I	R	A	E	■	D	A	N	S	K	■	■
M	I	L	L	E	R	■	■	■	M	O	O	R	E	■
U	S	E	R	S	F	E	E	S	■	I	P	A	D	S
G	E	T	I	T	■	U	S	H	E	R	E	D	I	N
G	R	O	G	S	■	R	A	I	L	■	N	I	N	A
Y	E	N	S	■	■	O	I	N	K	■	S	O	A	P

25

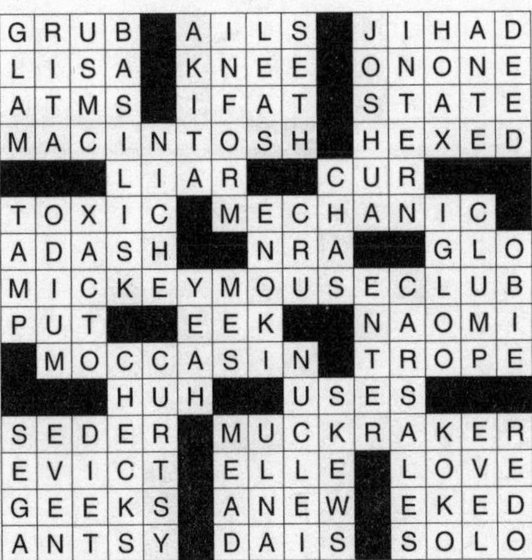

G	R	U	B	■	A	I	L	S	■	J	I	H	A	D
L	I	S	A	■	K	N	E	E	■	O	N	O	N	E
A	T	M	S	■	I	F	A	T	■	S	T	A	T	E
M	A	C	I	N	T	O	S	H	■	H	E	X	E	D
■	■	■	L	I	A	R	■	■	C	U	R	■	■	■
T	O	X	I	C	■	M	E	C	H	A	N	I	C	■
A	D	A	S	H	■	■	N	R	A	■	■	G	L	O
M	I	C	K	E	Y	M	O	U	S	E	C	L	U	B
P	U	T	■	■	E	E	K	■	■	N	A	O	M	I
■	M	O	C	C	A	S	I	N	■	T	R	O	P	E
■	■	■	H	U	H	■	■	U	S	E	S	■	■	■
S	E	D	E	R	■	M	U	C	K	R	A	K	E	R
E	V	I	C	T	■	E	L	L	E	■	L	O	V	E
G	E	E	K	S	■	A	N	E	W	■	E	K	E	D
A	N	T	S	Y	■	D	A	I	S	■	S	O	L	O

26

C	A	W	■	S	P	R	Y	■	P	U	S	H	I	T
A	V	E	■	Y	O	Y	O	■	E	S	P	A	N	A
R	I	A	■	S	W	E	D	I	S	H	F	I	S	H
L	A	S	S	■	■	B	A	S	T	E	■	R	P	I
S	T	E	A	M	E	R	■	B	O	R	O	D	I	N
J	E	L	L	Y	B	E	A	N	S	■	N	O	R	I
R	D	S	■	B	O	A	S	■	■	C	A	S	E	S
■	■	C	A	N	D	Y	C	O	R	N	■	■	■	■
S	T	R	A	D	■	■	E	A	V	E	■	E	G	G
T	W	I	N	■	H	O	T	T	A	M	A	L	E	S
P	O	S	T	M	A	N	■	E	L	E	M	E	N	T
E	T	S	■	A	B	Z	U	G	■	■	A	V	E	R
T	O	O	T	S	I	E	R	O	L	L	■	A	R	I
E	N	L	I	S	T	■	G	R	I	P	■	T	I	N
R	E	E	S	E	S	■	E	Y	E	S	■	E	C	G

27

W	O	L	F	M	A	N	■	N	A	M	F	L	O	W
I	N	U	T	E	R	O	■	A	R	I	G	A	T	O
M	O	N	S	T	E	R	■	R	E	T	S	N	O	M
P	R	E	M	I	U	M	■	N	A	T	■	D	E	B
■	■	■	I	M	P	■	M	I	S	E	R	■	■	■
S	K	A	T	E	■	V	I	A	■	N	O	T	S	O
L	O	C	H	■	J	A	R	■	J	S	B	A	C	H
O	A	T	■	■	A	T	R	I	A	■	■	C	A	Y
G	L	O	S	S	Y	■	O	R	B	■	E	I	N	E
S	A	R	A	H	■	A	R	K	■	P	U	T	T	S
■	■	■	D	I	A	L	S	■	S	A	G	■	■	■
A	C	C	■	A	B	U	■	I	N	S	E	C	T	S
P	H	A	N	T	O	M	■	M	O	T	N	A	H	P
E	A	S	E	S	I	N	■	S	W	E	E	P	E	A
D	R	A	C	U	L	A	■							

28

D	R	U	G	S	■	M	U	S	S	■	A	B	B	A
N	I	G	H	T	■	O	H	N	O	■	C	O	L	T
A	B	H	O	R	■	S	A	I	D	I	T	N	O	T
■	■	■	S	I	T	S	U	P	■	M	O	N	T	E
C	A	N	T	F	O	O	L	■	B	E	R	E	T	S
O	R	A	T	E	S	■	■	A	L	L	■	T	O	T
M	I	S	O	■	■	A	R	M	A	D	A	■	■	■
B	E	T	W	E	E	N	Y	O	U	A	N	D	M	E
■	■	■	N	A	N	T	E	S	■	■	Y	E	A	R
H	A	T	■	G	I	S	■	■	C	A	M	A	R	O
O	S	W	A	L	D	■	T	A	L	K	I	N	T	O
W	H	A	L	E	■	M	O	V	E	I	N	■	■	■
D	O	N	T	S	C	A	R	E	■	T	U	R	B	O
A	R	G	O	■	S	P	A	R	■	A	T	A	R	I
H	E	S	S	■	A	S	H	Y	■	S	E	G	A	L

29

R	I	A	T	A	S	■	S	H	A	M	■	F	B	I
A	N	T	E	U	P	■	W	O	V	E	■	A	L	F
R	H	O	N	D	A	■	ARMED	B	A	N	D	I	T	S
E	A	U	■	I	N	I	■	O	R	S	O	N	■	■
BIT	BIT	C	R	O	O	K	S	■	I	A	N	■	■	■
■	■	H	U	B	■	E	P	I	C	■	T	R	I	P
A	P	O	L	O	■	B	O	N	E	S	■	E	C	O
F	I	V	E	O	■	A	R	D	■	T	O	T	E	S
T	E	E	■	K	I	N	T	E	■	E	L	U	D	E
A	R	R	S	■	G	A	S	X	■	A	I	R	■	■
■	■	■	E	I	N	■	CARD	CARD	CARD	M	O	N	T	E
■	■	S	A	T	I	N	■	S	A	P	■	F	I	R
WAY	WAY	WAY	WAY	S	T	O	P	■	M	I	N	I	N	G
N	I	E	■	M	E	D	E	■	O	P	O	R	T	O
E	N	D	■	E	D	E	N	■	M	E	R	E	S	T

30

H	A	D	J	■	S	C	O	W	■	A	L	O	H	A
A	L	I	A	■	U	H	N	O	■	L	O	D	E	S
R	O	O	M	■	B	I	E	L	■	E	V	E	N	S
P	U	R	E	L	L	■	■	F	I	V	E	R	S	■
■	■	■	S	E	E	S	A	F	T	E	R	■	■	■
A	N	O	I	N	T	E	D	■	I	L	L	P	A	Y
F	E	L	I	D	■	R	O	A	N	■	Y	I	P	E
L	E	E	■	L	E	I	■	D	A	Y	■	E	L	O
A	D	I	A	■	S	E	E	M	■	A	F	L	O	W
C	Y	C	L	E	S	■	R	E	A	L	I	S	T	S
■	■	■	B	E	A	N	A	N	G	E	L	■	■	■
■	A	M	A	L	I	E	■	■	L	U	M	M	O	X
S	C	E	N	E	■	L	E	I	A	■	D	O	R	M
C	L	A	I	R	■	L	E	E	R	■	O	L	G	A
H	U	L	A	S	■	Y	O	R	E	■	M	E	S	S

31

S	C	A	B		S	E	A	M		S	H	A	S	T	A
H	O	U	R		A	X	L	E		T	O	W	A	R	D
I	P	S	O		W	I	L	L	B	E	B	L	O	O	D
N	I	T	W	I	T	S		V	A	I	O		T	O	R
G	O	E	S	N	O	T	H	I	N	G		P	O	P	E
L	U	R	E	S		E	I	N	E		G	A	M	E	S
E	S	E		T	A	N	G			C	R	I	E	R	S
			N	E	I	T	H	E	R	N	O	R			
S	T	R	E	A	M			R	E	N	U		M	E	W
C	H	A	R	D		R	A	I	D		C	H	A	C	O
R	E	I	D		C	O	M	E	S	T	H	E	S	U	N
E	R	N		K	O	F	I		C	O	O	L	C	A	T
W	A	S	A	N	O	L	D	M	A	N		D	A	D	O
I	G	O	T	I	T		S	O	R	E		T	R	O	N
T	E	N	E	T	S		T	I	E	D		O	A	R	S

32

H	E	P		S	H	I	R	K		A	D	E	L	A
A	A	A		A	U	D	I	O		D	O	D	O	S
M	V	P		S	H	I	P	P	E	D	G	I	F	T
S	E	E	P	S			A	P	R		F	E	T	A
		R	O	Y	A	L		E	L	I	A			
M	O	T	O		M	A	I	L	E	D	C	A	R	D
S	C	O	R	P	I	O	N			E	E	L	E	R
N	A	W		U	N	S	T	O	P	S		L	O	A
B	L	E	A	R			R	H	E	T	O	R	I	C
C	A	L	L	E	D	H	O	M	E		H	I	L	O
			L	E	I	A		E	R	R	O	L		
U	Z	I	S		A	R	K			U	S	E	R	S
S	E	N	T	F	L	O	W	E	R	S		D	E	P
C	A	C	A	O		L	A	V	E	S		U	A	R
G	L	A	R	E		D	I	A	N	E		P	R	Y

33

A	J	A	R		A	W	A	L	K		N	C	A	A
M	O	N	O		V	O	I	C	E	C	O	A	C	H
B	E	T	W	E	E	N	T	H	E	L	I	N	E	S
	C	O	S	Y				A	L	I	S	T	S	
S	O	I		R	I	C	C	I		E	Y	E	O	N
W	O	N	D	E	R	W	O	M	A	N		R	U	E
F	L	E	A		A	T	M		N	T	E	S	T	S
			H		I		M		O		M			
T	E	S	L	A	S		O	B	I		I	M	A	X
A	M	Y		L	E	A	D	I	N	G	L	A	D	Y
B	I	N	A	L		R	E	C	T	O		C	U	Z
	R	A	M	O	N	E				E	T	A	L	
H	A	P	P	Y	M	O	T	H	E	R	S	D	A	Y
I	T	S	U	S	E	L	E	S	S		K	A	T	E
P	E	E	P		X	A	X	I	S		S	M	E	W

34

C	A	T	S		A	L	I	S	T		L	A	V	A
U	N	U	M		R	A	C	K	S		E	D	E	N
S	T	R	O	N	G	W	E	E	K		F	O	N	T
P	I	N	T	O				I	T	S	T	R	U	E
			H	I	D	D	E	N	S	C	E	N	E	
N	A	M	E	D	R	O	P		K	A	Y			
A	V	E	R		N	E	I	N		P	E	S	K	Y
Z	I	T		L	O	S	T	O	N	E		L	A	S
I	D	A	H	O		T	O	T	O		W	A	N	E
			E	C	K		M	U	L	L	O	V	E	R
	B	R	A	K	E	R	E	P	A	I	R			
N	A	I	V	E	T	E				M	S	N	B	C
O	B	O	E		T	H	E	Y	R	E	H	E	R	E
M	E	T	H		L	A	N	A	I		I	R	A	N
E	S	S	O		E	B	O	O	K		P	O	N	T

35

	D	I	N	E		T	E	E	M		F	O	R	K	S
	J	O	E	L		H	A	L	O		A	N	N	I	E
	E	T	A	L		E	C	H	O		L	L	A	M	A
MAN	D	A	R	I	N	C	H	I	N	E	S	E			
				O	O	H				L	E	A	N	T	O
MAN	U	A	L	T	R	A	N	S	M	I	S	S	I	O	N
	L	S	A	T		M	O	T	O		T	H	E	S	E
	L	I	T			P	I	O	U	S			K	S	U
	M	A	T	T	E		R	I	N	K		D	R	I	P
MAN	A	G	E	E	X	P	E	C	T	A	T	I	O	N	S
	N	O	N	A	M	E				G	U	V			
				M	A	N	O	V	E	R	B	O	A	R	D
	I	T	G	U	Y		Z	E	R	O		R	U	B	E
	Q	U	E	S	O		M	E	N	U		C	R	I	B
	S	M	E	A	R		A	P	O	P		E	A	S	T

36

R	U	M	B	A	■	P	R	E	Z	■	G	N	A	T
A	L	O	O	N	■	R	O	L	E	■	R	I	L	E
K	N	O	X	K	N	O	C	K	S	■	A	X	E	R
E	A	R	S	H	O	T	■	S	T	I	N	K	E	R
■	R	E	E	■	M	E	M	■	A	N	O	N	■	■
■	■	■	A	R	A	M	I	S	■	A	L	I	S	T
D	A	R	T	E	D	■	T	A	X	T	A	C	K	S
O	R	E	■	T	I	P	O	V	E	R	■	K	E	A
L	O	X	L	O	C	K	S	■	R	E	I	S	E	R
T	O	W	I	T	■	G	I	J	O	E	S	■	■	■
■	■	R	E	A	M	■	S	I	X	■	O	M	E	■
I	C	E	F	L	O	E	■	N	E	T	L	O	S	S
M	C	C	L	■	S	T	A	X	S	T	A	C	K	S
A	N	K	A	■	S	T	Y	E	■	O	T	H	E	R
M	Y	S	T	■	Y	A	R	D	■	P	E	A	R	S

37

M	E	Y	E	R	■	■	S	E	T	H	■	L	B	J
I	(R)	(E)	(N)	A	■	T	H	R	E	E	Y	E	A	R
M	A	C	Y	S	■	R	A	I	L	(R)	(O)	(A)	D	S
I	T	H	A	S	C	I	R	C	L	E	S	■	■	■
■	■	■	■	L	U	M	P	■	■	■	T	O	R	Y
A	L	G	I	E	R	S	■	M	C	S	■	T	H	E
T	E	A	S	■	■	■	A	G	I	T	A	T	O	R
M	A	Y	B	E	Y	E	S	M	A	Y	B	E	N	O
F	R	E	N	(Z)	(I)	(E)	S	■	■	■	U	R	D	U
E	N	S	■	R	N	S	■	H	I	N	T	S	A	T
E	S	T	H	■	■	■	F	E	T	A	■	■	■	■
■	■	■	U	N	D	E	R	I	T	S	E	Y	E	S
L	A	U	R	E	A	T	E	S	■	C	(R)	(E)	(A)	K
V	O	L	L	E	Y	E	R	S	■	A	M	O	R	Y
I	L	E	■	(D)	(O)	(S)	E	■	■	R	A	W	L	S

38

W	H	O	■	S	A	W	Y	E	R	■	R	I	C	H
H	A	T	■	C	R	E	O	L	E	■	E	S	A	U
E	N	O	■	H	A	N	D	E	L	■	J	U	S	T
E	D	S	E	L	■	T	A	C	O	■	O	R	E	S
■	■	■	B	E	S	T	■	T	A	P	I	R	■	■
M	E	T	A	P	H	O	R	■	D	E	C	E	I	T
O	P	R	Y	■	O	P	U	S	■	L	E	N	N	Y
V	O	A	■	T	W	O	B	A	L	L	■	D	I	N
E	D	I	F	Y	■	T	I	T	I	■	S	E	G	A
S	E	L	E	C	T	■	N	I	N	E	I	R	O	N
■	■	B	R	O	O	D	■	N	E	X	T	■	■	■
A	V	I	V	■	S	O	L	D	■	C	H	O	W	S
T	A	K	E	■	S	N	O	O	Z	E	■	G	A	P
L	I	E	N	■	E	A	G	L	E	S	■	L	I	E
I	N	S	T	■	S	T	Y	L	E	S	■	E	T	C

39

B	A	H	S	■	S	C	A	R	F	■	B	A	D	E
O	L	E	O	■	T	I	M	O	R	■	I	L	E	R
W	O	L	F	D	N	A	B	B	E	■	G	I	T	A
L	E	D	T	O	■	■	L	O	S	L	O	B	O	S
■	■	W	E	I	V	R	E	T	N	I	T	I	X	E
J	E	A	N	N	I	E	■	S	O	A	R	■	■	■
A	L	T	■	■	N	A	P	■	■	N	Y	L	O	N
C	H	E	■	W	O	R	C	T	A	E	■	I	V	E
K	I	R	B	Y	■	■	S	E	C	■	■	F	E	W
■	■	■	E	L	A	N	■	N	E	U	T	E	R	S
W	O	N	T	I	S	E	O	D	Y	S	A	E	■	■
O	M	A	R	E	P	P	S	■	■	D	I	V	A	S
V	E	G	A	■	E	A	S	T	T	O	W	E	S	T
E	G	G	Y	■	C	L	I	O	S	■	A	N	K	A
N	A	Y	S	■	T	I	E	T	O	■	N	T	S	B

40

J	I	B	S	■	P	E	R	O	T	■	S	H	E	D
E	M	U	S	■	E	R	I	C	H	■	A	E	R	O
T	H	E	R	E	S	N	O	T	E	L	L	I	N	G
S	I	N	■	L	E	E	S	■	D	E	E	R	E	S
■	P	O	S	I	T	S	■	■	O	N	S	■	■	■
■	■	■	T	H	A	T	S	N	O	T	T	R	U	E
P	A	L	A	U	■	■	H	A	R	■	A	U	R	A
A	M	O	F	■	G	L	A	S	S	■	R	E	G	S
R	O	L	F	■	U	A	L	■	■	A	G	R	E	E
T	I	L	L	N	E	X	T	T	I	M	E	■	■	■
■	■	■	O	Y	S	■	■	O	N	A	T	I	P	■
N	O	F	U	S	S	■	G	R	A	N	■	S	E	S
T	H	E	N	E	W	T	E	S	T	A	M	E	N	T
W	I	N	G	■	H	A	N	O	I	■	L	E	I	A
T	O	N	E	■	O	B	E	S	E	■	B	A	N	G

41

E	S	E	■	P	I	S	A	■	I	S	W	E	A	R
C	O	N	C	E	D	E	D	■	S	P	E	L	L	O
A	R	T	I	C	L	E	S	■	L	A	N	D	A	U
S	T	R	I	K	E	O	■	S	A	W	T	O	I	T
H	O	E	■	■	■	U	P	C	■	N	O	R	■	■
■	F	E	R	R	E	T	S	O	■	■	N	A	P	S
■	■	■	O	E	D	■	S	U	E	T	■	D	I	P
T	E	E	N	A	G	E	■	T	R	I	L	O	G	Y
I	R	S	■	M	E	S	A	■	N	E	A	■	■	■
T	A	C	O	■	■	P	A	P	E	R	B	A	G	■
■	■	A	R	E	■	Y	A	O	■	■	■	N	O	I
A	S	P	E	C	T	S	■	T	E	A	R	O	O	M
C	H	I	L	L	O	■	F	A	L	L	I	N	G	O
N	A	S	S	A	U	■	I	T	O	L	D	Y	O	U
E	M	M	E	T	T	■	T	O	N	Y	■	M	O	T

42

P	O	N	C	E	■	T	V	A	D	■	L	U	S	T
A	D	I	O	S	■	R	A	M	S	■	I	T	T	O
C	O	C	O	C	H	A	N	E	L	■	M	I	E	N
T	R	E	K	■	O	D	I	N	■	D	E	C	A	Y
■	■	■	I	M	P	E	L	■	O	O	L	A	L	A
A	N	G	E	R	S	■	L	E	D	G	E	■	■	■
G	U	E	S	S	■	K	A	T	E	S	M	I	T	H
E	D	N	A	■	L	A	M	A	S	■	O	M	O	O
S	E	E	N	O	E	V	I	L	■	S	N	O	R	E
■	■	■	D	I	V	A	N	■	B	R	O	K	E	R
M	U	S	C	L	Y	■	T	H	E	I	R	■	■	■
U	S	E	R	S	■	N	C	A	A	■	A	I	N	T
N	A	T	E	■	J	O	H	N	D	E	N	V	E	R
R	I	T	A	■	A	V	I	D	■	A	G	A	T	E
O	R	E	M	■	M	A	P	S	■	T	E	N	S	E

43

A	D	O	■	E	S	P	N	■	I	R	O	B	O	T
R	I	G	■	A	L	O	E	■	D	E	J	A	V	U
C	A	R	T	R	I	P	S	■	E	G	O	Y	A	N
■	Z	E	E	■	M	U	T	T	E	R	■	O	L	E
■	■	■	C	U	S	P	■	I	S	I	N	F	O	R
L	O	C	H	S	■	T	L	C	■	P	U	F	F	■
A	P	R	■	S	N	O	O	K	I	■	B	U	F	F
L	E	A	■	R	E	A	R	E	N	D	■	N	I	A
O	N	C	E	■	T	S	E	T	S	E	■	D	C	I
■	S	K	E	E	■	T	N	T	■	F	R	Y	E	R
G	O	E	S	A	P	E	■	O	T	T	O	■	■	■
I	U	D	■	S	A	R	T	R	E	■	L	O	A	■
G	R	I	P	E	S	■	W	I	N	D	O	W	S	8
O	C	C	U	L	T	■	O	D	O	R	■	E	T	A
T	E	E	N	S	Y	■	D	E	N	Y	■	D	I	M

44

G	I	J	O	E	■	A	M	A	S	S	■	A	M	P
I	S	E	R	E	■	R	A	L	P	H	■	G	A	L
F	R	A	N	K	L	I	N	I	O	O	■	E	R	A
■	■	N	A	S	A	■	■	B	I	O	L	O	G	Y
A	B	A	T	■	H	A	M	I	L	T	O	N	I	O
C	L	U	E	S	■	R	R	S	■	■	T	E	N	N
T	O	E	■	E	X	A	M	■	A	L	T	■	■	■
■	C	L	E	V	E	L	A	N	D	I	O	O	O	■
■	■	■	R	E	D	■	G	A	Z	E	■	L	G	A
O	S	S	O	■	■	P	O	T	■	D	R	I	L	L
C	H	A	S	E	I	O	O	O	O	■	A	V	E	S
C	A	V	E	R	N	S	■	■	W	A	G	E	■	■
U	K	E	■	W	A	S	H	I	N	G	T	O	N	I
P	E	A	■	I	N	U	I	T	■	F	O	Y	E	R
Y	R	S	■	N	E	M	E	A	■	A	P	L	U	S

45

P	O	O	R	■	P	O	O	L	■	■	P	O	L	L
E	I	R	E	■	I	M	N	O	■	C	O	K	I	E
L	L	B	S	■	M	A	T	S	■	A	K	E	L	A
O	C	A	■	C	A	R	O	■	F	R	E	Y	A	■
S	A	C	R	A	■	■	P	O	L	E	■	D	B	L
I	N	H	I	B	I	T	■	N	O	T	D	O	N	E
■	■	■	N	O	N	U	S	E	R	■	U	K	E	S
■	I	N	S	T	A	N	T	W	I	N	N	E	R	■
K	N	E	E	■	K	N	E	A	D	E	D	■	■	■
I	F	O	R	O	N	E	■	Y	A	L	E	M	A	N
X	I	N	■	R	O	L	E	■	■	L	E	I	C	A
■	N	A	G	A	T	■	C	I	T	Y	■	D	E	M
B	I	T	A	T	■	M	O	M	A	■	N	O	T	A
A	T	A	L	E	■	A	L	A	S	■	C	R	I	T
R	I	L	E	■	■	R	I	C	E	■	R	I	C	H

46

ASTRA HEAVE NOG
BEHAR ASKEW ORE
EXITRAMPAGE RAY
NEILL LAWNS
ICK DIETPILLAGE
KOBE THIN DYER
ELIXIR ELUDE
AGEDIFFERENCE
CAPRI ELTORO
BEAU EARP ENID
INSTANTMESS CEE
OTHER APPLE
NIL MUSICALPASS
IRE ENOCH IGLOO
CEY DOPEY TASTY

47

BRAN BEATLE ADD
RUTS ARTHUR LEO
ABBY TITANS MSN
GIANTSQUID FAME
SKYCAM ENERO
CARDINALSIN
DADA NEAR PLANO
OLINS AKA SALES
SLADE CANS SASE
TIGERSTRIPE
SNAFU AXIOMS
KWON PIRATESHIP
NES DEVITO LANE
ELI ERESTU ERIN
ELS ABSENT TEST

48

SHAFT BLIP PRET
AIDAN OONA LALA
PRINTSOFTHIEVES
SENT PITH NAIVE
AGIN EMUS
LOSINGPATIENTS
SELIG LINT OBE
UCLA YOURS TWIX
MAI LANG HAIRY
PRESENTSOFMIND
WIKI IDOL
ATTIC POLI GIGI
JUMPATTHECHANTS
ATEE VOIR STOOL
RUNS GEOS TENSE

49

HULA HOFF SLOTH
OHOS ORAL CANWE
SUCKS 2B YOU AFTER
PHOENIX 2B ALOVER
DOT SEDER
TAXI HERE GAEA
OPENAREA SEEMS 2B
MAN 2B ORNOT 2B ITO
BRIDE 2B CHESSSET
STAR EWES CHET
YPRES APR
2B HONEST BRIEFED
GOMER BORN 2B WILD
UMASS ARIA ISSA
NORSE RITZ THEY

50

RADS CAPED PSST
ESAU IVANI ETTA
DOANDROIDSDREAM
OFELECTRICSHEEP
ABLEST CALLA
COMMIE ASP
ERUPT BUMP SPIN
RAT SAMPLED ODE
FLEA DICK ADULT
RID TNOTES
ALARM PIGOUT
WECANREMEMBERIT
FORYOUWHOLESALE
UNIE HEIDI ORYX
LADD REPEN NEAT

51

B L U E C R A B ■ L O W F A T
O I L S H A L E ■ B R O O C H
N O N T I T L E ■ J I L T E E
D N A ■ ■ T O R T R E F O R M
■ ■ ■ C L A W C R A N E ■ ■ ■
P A T R O N S A I N T ■ A S A
E B O O K ■ ■ N E C ■ R C A S
T A R N I S H ■ S H T E T L S
A C M E ■ M A O ■ ■ R A I T T
L I E ■ V E L V E T E L V I S
■ ■ ■ F A L L E N H E M ■ ■ ■
E L D O C T O R O W ■ ■ V F W
C O U G A R ■ B R A S S E R A
O R S I N O ■ I M R U I N E D
N I E N T E ■ D E T E N T E S

52

S Q U A B B L E ■ J A M C A M
E U P H O R I A ■ O R I O L E
T I P S H E E T ■ K I D U L T
B B S ■ M A L I C E ■ E L S E
A B A S ■ K O T O ■ H A D T O
I L L I N ■ W U N D E R B A R
L E A N O N ■ P I E R ■ E R S
■ ■ ■ S O U P ■ C L O P ■ ■ ■
S E A ■ G T O S ■ L I T O U T
E X Q U I S I T E ■ C A N S O
A T U N E ■ S U C H ■ S E T T
G R I P ■ D E C A Y S ■ M I A
R E V I S E ■ K R A T I O N S
A M E L I E ■ U T T E R R O T
M E R E S T ■ P E T P E E V E

53

■ ■ D A R E S S A L A A M ■ ■
■ C O N T A C T L E N S E S ■
W H A T S T H E B I G D E A L
R O S H ■ A N T E ■ ■ F R I A
A L I E N T O ■ I N F ■ K N T
P E D R O ■ O S T E O P A T H
S R O ■ N U K E ■ A R E T E S
■ ■ ■ T O P S E C R E T ■ ■ ■
S A R D I S ■ T O S S ■ O Y E
P R E S S E S O N ■ E R T E S
E F S ■ E T O ■ C H E E T O S
N A T E ■ ■ B R E A ■ T A M A
T R Y T O S E E I T M Y W A Y
■ F L A S H I N T H E P A N ■
■ ■ E S T A T E S A L E S ■ ■

54

B U T T D I A L E D ■ G I B E
O N A R A M P A G E ■ U N O S
T I D A L B A S I N ■ M O B S
S T A P L E R ■ S A C ■ N S A
■ ■ ■ P A C T S ■ L O V E L Y
I C E ■ S I M I ■ I N A P E T
N A N S ■ L E T S ■ A S I D E
B R I E F E N C O U N T E R S
A D D E R ■ T O R N ■ S C U T
D E B T E E ■ M E I N ■ E N S
S A L O O N ■ S L O O P ■ ■ ■
O L Y ■ N A M ■ O N S E R V E
R E T D ■ C A S S I O P E I A
T R O Y ■ T A K E S A S E A T
S S N S ■ S M A R T P I L L S

55

Y I D D I S H ■ A I R M A I L
A R I A N N A ■ C L E A N S E
W I S H F U L D R I N K I N G
E N B L O C ■ E Y E T E S T S
D A E ■ ■ K F C ■ D A G ■ ■ ■
■ ■ L A E ■ A A H ■ ■ O S H A
T W I T T E R F O L L O W E R
O N E T O G O ■ P A Y D I R T
S E V E N O F D I A M O N D S
S T E N ■ ■ F E N ■ E N G ■ ■
■ ■ ■ D E T ■ A G O ■ ■ F U R
T R I A X I A L ■ W I N O N A
M I D N I G H T I N P A R I S
E L E C T R A ■ D E S P I T E
N E M E S E S ■ O R E S T E S

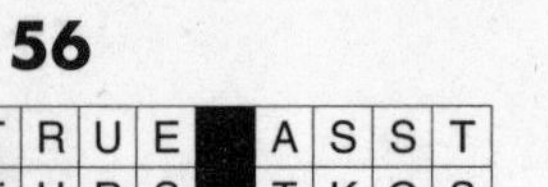

56

T	H	I	S	I	S	T	R	U	E		A	S	S	T
R	A	C	O	N	T	E	U	R	S		T	K	O	S
I	N	A	R	T	I	S	T	I	C		T	A	L	K
C	E	N	T	E	R	S			R	I	A	T	A	S
E	S	T	E	R			H	O	O	S	I	E	R	
			R	I	P	V	A	N	W	I	N	K	L	E
A	N	I		M	A	U	V	E		S	T	E	A	L
L	A	M	B		C	L	A	S	H		S	Y	M	S
A	T	P	A	R		C	R	E	E	D		S	P	A
N	U	R	S	E	R	A	T	C	H	E	D			
	R	O	S	S	I	N	I			S	E	L	M	A
C	A	V	I	T	Y			R	A	I	S	E	U	P
O	L	I	N		A	N	N	E	B	R	O	N	T	E
E	L	S	E		D	E	A	D	L	E	T	T	E	R
N	Y	E	T		H	O	W	D	Y	D	O	O	D	Y

57

R	E	S	T	A	I	N				C	O	M	E	T	S
O	S	C	A	R	N	O	D	S		O	P	A	Q	U	E
S	T	O	R	Y	B	O	O	K		B	A	K	U	L	A
Y	O	W	Z	A		K	N	O	W		L	E	A	S	T
			A	N	S		T	R	I	B		A	L	A	S
	V	O	N		M	S	T		N	A	T	S			
L	I	T	T	L	E	L	E	A	G	U	E	T	E	A	M
I	S	T	H	A	T	A	L	L	T	H	E	R	E	I	S
B	A	S	E	B	A	L	L	D	I	A	M	O	N	D	S
			A	S	N	O		A	P	U		N	Y	E	
W	A	S	P		A	M	F	M		S	K	G			
A	S	H	E	S		S	O	A	K		A	C	O	A	T
I	S	O	M	E	R		A	T	A	G	L	A	N	C	E
T	E	J	A	N	O		M	O	V	I	E	S	E	T	S
S	T	I	N	G	Y				A	L	L	E	G	E	S

58

D	R	A	W	E	R		B	A	S	I	L	I	C	A
R	E	M	O	R	A		A	R	C	H	I	V	A	L
E	L	I	J	A	H		H	A	R	A	K	I	R	I
W	O	R	T		M	A	I	M		V	E	E	P	S
A	S	S	Y	R		S	A	I	L	E	D			
			L	O	T	T		S	A	N	T	A	N	A
P	A	R	A	G	U	A	Y		M	O	O	C	O	W
O	R	E		U	R	B	A	N	I	I		I	V	A
R	I	E	S	E	N		W	I	N	D	Y	D	A	Y
T	A	K	E	S	T	O		G	A	E	A			
			A	T	O	N	C	E		A	N	D	E	S
S	A	S	H	A		F	O	R	T		G	R	A	M
L	O	C	A	T	I	O	N		R	A	T	I	T	E
E	N	I	W	E	T	O	K		E	C	Z	E	M	A
D	E	S	K	S	E	T	S		F	E	E	D	E	R

LEFT PORT, RIGHT AWAY, BOTTOM FEEDER, TOP-DRAWER

59

C	R	A	Z	I	E	R			A	B	B	O	T	S
A	U	G	U	S	T	U	S		B	A	L	B	O	A
C	S	I	M	I	A	M	I		C	M	A	J	O	R
A	T	L	A	S		B	L	T	S		M	E	L	C
O	Y	E			L	A	I	R		M	E	C	C	A
			M	A	E		C	U	T	E		T	A	S
		P	O	S	T	M	O	D	E	R	N	I	S	M
	D	R	S	T	R	A	N	G	E	L	O	V	E	
D	E	A	T	H	I	N	V	E	N	I	C	E		
O	M	G		M	P	A	A		I	N	K			
M	O	M	M	A		G	L	E	E			S	A	C
I	T	A	S		F	E	L	L		S	M	I	T	E
N	A	T	T	E	R		E	I	T	H	E	R	O	R
O	P	I	A	T	E		Y	O	U	O	W	E	M	E
S	E	C	R	E	T			T	O	P	L	E	S	S

60

A	V	A	I	L	A	B	L	E	C	R	E	D	I	T
P	E	R	C	E	N	T	A	G	E	E	R	R	O	R
E	N	T	E	N	T	E	C	O	R	D	I	A	L	E
S	T	A	R	S	I	N	O	N	E	S	E	Y	E	S
			S	E	T		N	S	A					
J	A	W		S	A	K	I		L	A	C	K	E	Y
A	T	A	D		N	A	C	L		M	I	L	N	E
M	R	L	U	C	K	Y		O	C	A	N	A	D	A
B	I	D	E	S		E	M	I	L		Q	U	I	T
S	P	O	T	T	V		O	N	E	D		S	T	S
					A	T	O		A	E	C			
A	M	E	R	I	C	A	N	I	N	P	A	R	I	S
R	E	G	U	L	A	R	G	A	S	O	L	I	N	E
F	E	E	D	I	N	G	O	N	E	S	F	A	C	E
S	T	R	E	E	T	A	D	D	R	E	S	S	E	S

61

ASBIG HST TOPUP
STORE OOH HYENA
HASANINTERESTIN
IRT ELK SOS ROD
PROCRASTINATING
NEA OZS HEF
GASOLINESTATION
MAT EKE TAR ERA
CARELESSABANDON
ATE HIT DEF
RANACLOSESECOND
ENG TOR MAS ROO
TOLERANCELEVELS
ALEXI ARN ROSIE
PEREC TOT TATER

62

PURPLEHAZE HSIA
UNDECLARED ATOP
STANDALONE BANS
HOSS TOD HORSE
IDEE CHAOS
DAVIDSTEINBERG
LINEA WELD AAR
ING LACOSTE RNA
EEL SLIT DECAF
DROPOUTOFSIGHT
SHAME LUNG
SHARP SIR RBIS
HEXA POWERPOINT
EROS IMAREALBOY
DONE PATSYCLINE

63

AMIWRONG JULIE
GAMEOVER SONATA
EXHIBITA ONAPAR
NOUS DIVINGBELL
DURST ZITI ALIG
ATT ACETEN SPAR
EPONYM THINE
AMEXES TEENSY
DAVID MEOWED
ARES CANNON MAT
PINT ONIT SLUSH
TAKEFLIGHT ARCO
SCENEI MERRYMEN
THECAN AQUALUNG
OILER STEWARDS

64

CREEPSHOW OXBOW
HURRICANE LARGE
OPENLANES INALL
REC ANDI EVADED
DETESTED XED
OPT LASCRUCES
BURIED STE OLE
UNSCREW UPRIGHT
RTE MAB TETRIS
BOTTLECAP TEA
VIA NEARMISS
POLLEN DEMO LEI
AREAS BIKINIWAX
LEANT ATANYRATE
MONDO SOTOMAYOR

65

CATSPAW EMAILED
ONATEAR MISSIVE
MAKETHEBESTOFIT
EGER SNARER ENO
DRANK LYRA ICU
UAL OPEL LASER
EMO BETTYS IVS
OVERTHEEDGE
TKO TEETER RCT
BRANS JIMI YAO
UAR USNA BASRA
MIO ICICLE RHOS
PLUMTUCKEREDOUT
PENROSE DIVERSE
ORDERIN SCENTED

66

IPHONEAPP■DCUPS

MROLYMPIA■ERNIE

PETEACHER■SEGER

UMS■HEIR■■■DATE

MITE■EDSULLIVAN

PEON■■■■NASTASE

ERNE■SPLINTS■■■

DEER■TRITE■COBB

■■■GROOVES■OPAL

ONLYYOU■■■■RENE

LOADEDDICE■ENNE

IBAR■■■OAST■TED

VALID■CURSEWORD

ELAND■ASIANPEAR

SLAKE■BABYDADDY

67

YAWN■STAB■■LIES

ECHO■TOUR■LADLE

CHARLESDEGAULLE

COMMERCIALBREAK

HOSANNA■COOED■■

■■■RIO■PHARLAP■

DIVAN■WAITS■WEB

EPEE■CHINS■CANE

WAN■SLANG■DAYNE

■DESPITE■GEL■■■

■■ZALES■PANACEA

YOUCANTWINEMALL

EVERYTHINGBAGEL

GALES■ANTE■RENO

GLAD■■TEAS■ISAY

68

SALADBAR■BAOBAB

ADEQUATE■ESSENE

VUVUZELA■CASITA

ELEA■ZILCH■ONIT

STEPS■■TREE■ESP

■■■LOUDOUTS■REO

DISASTERS■TORRE

EMANUEL■HEADOUT

ANNEE■ICESTORMS

ROT■MULEDEER■■■

MTA■ELAL■■SEEYA

AHAB■THICK■ALER

DENALI■CONSTANT

ARNHEM■ALIMENTS

MEANTO■SATURDAY

69

TABLECLOTH■SEGA

MIRACLEGRO■MARS

AMYPOEHLER■ARES

NEN■■AMENRA■LGA

■■■ESTA■DON■MAI

POSTMEN■IRT■ORL

OPENED■INSIGNIA

RENAL■ROG■BORON

TRESTLES■BOWOUT

LAG■REA■OLDNESS

ATA■OED■PAYS■■■

NIL■EROTIC■■PHD

DOES■SNEAKAPEEK

INSP■ALLTERRAIN

ASEA■TYLERPERRY

70

INSTAMATIC■THAN

DOORTODOOR■REPO

IMPATIENCE■YAPS

GES■ISLE■DEFTLY

■■■TREE■REWOVE■

AGREES■SENORITA

GOONS■SPECK■SIP

ATTN■STILE■TINT

SHO■APRES■REOIL

PARALLEL■TEENSY

■MOCKUP■MEDS■■■

ECOCAR■DOFF■ZIP

SITU■GUILLOTINE

STES■EASTORANGE

EYRE■SECONDGEAR

71

S	N	A	I	L	S	H	E	L	L		A	P	E	D
H	A	R	R	Y	C	A	R	A	Y		X	O	X	O
E	S	C	A	L	A	T	O	R	S		E	L	I	A
A	S	H	I	E	R			Y	E	S	L	E	T	S
T	A	I	L	S		Q	A	N	D	A		A	L	I
H	U	E	S		S	T	Y	X		X	A	X	I	S
				S	P	I	N		L	O	R	E	N	A
B	O	X	S	T	E	P		W	I	N	F	R	E	Y
U	S	E	T	A	X		Z	A	N	Y				
M	O	R	A	N		T	E	N	T		R	E	B	A
P	L	O		C	L	U	E	D		B	E	T	E	L
S	E	X	S	H	O	P			S	A	S	H	A	Y
O	M	I	T		W	E	B	B	A	N	N	E	R	S
F	I	N	D		P	L	A	I	N	J	A	N	E	S
F	O	G	S		H	O	R	S	E	O	P	E	R	A

72

	C	H	A	P						P	R	I	M	
V	O	I	C	E	D				S	E	E	G	E	R
L	E	T	T	E	R	C		S	T	E	A	N	N	E
O	U	T	S	K	I	P		H	U	R	L	I	N	G
G	R	I	M	I	E	R		A	D	S	I	T	E	S
	S	T	A	N	D	T	O	R	E	A	S	O	N	
		E	D	G	A	R	W	I	N	T	E	R		
					P	A	I	N	T					
		H	E	A	R	I	N	G	D	O	G	S		
	H	A	N	G	I	N	G	A	R	O	U	N	D	
L	A	T	T	I	C	E		B	I	L	L	E	R	S
E	V	E	R	T	O	R		E	V	I	L	E	Y	E
N	O	S	E	A	T	S		D	E	T	E	R	G	E
O	C	T	E	T	S				R	E	T	E	A	M
	S	O	S	O						S	S	R	S	

73

S	A	N	T	A	N	A		N	E	T	F	L	I	X
C	H	U	N	N	E	L		O	X	I	D	A	T	E
A	I	R	T	A	X	I		S	P	R	A	Y	E	R
L	T	S		G	U	M	S	H	O	E		A	M	O
D	U	E	T		S	O	L	O	S		T	W	I	X
E	N	R	O	N		N	O	W		G	R	A	Z	E
D	A	Y	L	I	L	Y		S	P	L	A	Y	E	D
			K	E	Y				D	I	P			
E	T	A	I	L	E	D		I	Q	T	E	S	T	S
N	O	T	E	S		I	N	C		Z	Z	T	O	P
C	O	E	N		I	V	I	E	S		E	U	R	E
A	S	I		A	M	O	E	B	A	S		N	N	E
M	O	N	S	T	E	R		A	M	I	S	T	A	D
P	O	T	O	M	A	C		T	O	R	P	E	D	O
S	N	O	C	O	N	E		H	A	I	R	D	O	S

74

A	C	T	F	I	V	E		O	F	F	C	A	S	T
F	A	I	R	B	A	N	K	S	A	L	A	S	K	A
F	R	E	E	A	S	S	O	C	I	A	T	I	O	N
A	L	G	O	R	E		M	A	N	X		M	P	G
B	E	A	N	S		P	O	R	T		M	O	J	O
L	A	M	S		B	U	D	S		L	O	V	E	S
E	S	E		B	R	N	O		R	O	O			
	E	S	P	R	I	T	D	E	C	O	R	P	S	
			A	I	M		R	A	M	P		L	I	D
S	K	O	R	T		H	A	S	P		N	O	L	O
A	A	H	S		S	A	G	E		J	A	W	E	D
I	B	M		Z	E	R	O		D	U	P	I	N	G
D	O	Y	O	U	W	A	N	N	A	D	A	N	C	E
H	O	M	E	L	E	S	S	S	H	E	L	T	E	R
I	M	Y	O	U	R	S		C	L	A	M	O	R	S

75

F	A	W	N		A	B	B	A		T	A	S	K	S
E	C	H	O		H	E	A	R		I	R	E	N	E
M	E	A	T	T	H	E	R	M	O	M	E	T	E	R
A	S	T	A	R		T	R	Y	M	E		T	W	A
		H	R	A	P			S	A	G	A	L		
P	L	A	Y	M	E	O	R	T	R	A	D	E	M	E
S	A	P		S	O	X	E	R		P	I	S	A	N
E	S	P	O		N	Y	T	O	L		A	T	N	O
U	S	E	A	S		G	I	N	O	S		H	O	T
D	O	N	T	E	V	E	N	G	O	T	H	E	R	E
		S	H	E	E	N			P	I	E	S		
C	T	N		K	E	A	T	S		L	Y	C	E	E
W	H	E	R	E	S	T	H	E	R	E	M	O	T	E
T	A	X	E	R		E	U	R	O		A	R	A	L
S	I	T	E	S		D	R	E	W		N	E	T	S

The New York Times

Crossword Puzzles

The #1 Name in Crosswords

Available at your local bookstore or online at nytimes.com/nytstore

Coming Soon!

Will Shortz Presents A Year of Crosswords	978-1-250-04487-7
Curious Crosswords	978-1-250-04488-4
More Monday Crossword Puzzles Omnibus Vol. 2	978-1-250-04493-8
More Tuesday Crossword Puzzles Omnibus Vol. 2	978-1-250-04494-5
Bedside Crosswords	978-1-250-04490-7
Crosswords to Supercharge Your Brainpower	978-1-250-04491-4
Best of Sunday Crosswords	978-1-250-04492-1
Teatime Crosswords	978-1-250-04489-1
Easy Crossword Puzzles Volume 15	978-1-250-04486-0
Soothing Sunday Crosswords	978-1-250-03917-0
Winter Wonderland Crosswords	978-1-250-03919-4
Best of Wednesday Crosswords	978-1-250-03913-2
Best of Thursday Crosswords	978-1-250-03912-5
Pocket-Size Puzzles: Crosswords	978-1-250-03915-6
Sunday Crosswords Volume 39	978-1-250-03918-7

Special Editions

Will Shortz Picks His Favorite Puzzles	978-0-312-64550-2
Crosswords for the Holidays	978-0-312-64544-1
Crossword Lovers Only: Easy Puzzles	978-0-312-54619-9
Crossword Lovers Only: Easy to Hard Puzzles	978-0-312-68139-5
Little Black & White Book of Holiday Crosswords	978-0-312-65424-5
Little Black (and White) Book of Sunday Crosswords	978-0-312-59003-1
Will Shortz's Wittiest, Wackiest Crosswords	978-0-312-59034-5
Crosswords to Keep Your Brain Young	978-0-312-37658-8
Little Black (and White) Book of Crosswords	978-0-312-36105-1
Little Flip Book of Crosswords	978-0-312-37043-5
Will Shortz's Favorite Crossword Puzzles	978-0-312-30613-7
Will Shortz's Favorite Sunday Crossword Puzzles	978-0-312-32488-9
Will Shortz's Greatest Hits	978-0-312-34242-5
Will Shortz Presents Crosswords for 365 Days	978-0-312-36121-1
Will Shortz's Funniest Crossword Puzzles	978-0-312-32489-8

Easy Crosswords

Easy Crossword Puzzles Vol. 13	978-1-250-00403-1
Easy Crossword Puzzle Volume 14	978-1-250-02520-3

Volumes 2–12 also available

Tough Crosswords

Tough Crossword Puzzles Vol. 13	978-0-312-34240-3
Tough Crossword Puzzles Vol. 12	978-0-312-32442-1

Volumes 9–11 also available

Sunday Crosswords

Sweet Sunday Crosswords	978-1-250-01592-6
Sunday Crosswords Puzzles Vol. 38	978-1-250-01544-0
Sunday in the Surf Crosswords	978-1-250-00924-1
Simply Sundays	978-1-250-00390-4
Fireside Sunday Crosswords	978-0-312-64546-5
Snuggle Up Sunday Crosswords	978-0-312-59057-4
Stay in Bed Sunday Crosswords	978-0-312-68144-9
Relaxing Sunday Crosswords	978-0-312-65429-0
Finally Sunday Crosswords	978-0-312-64113-9
Crosswords for a Lazy Sunday	978-0-312-60820-0
Sunday's Best	978-0-312-37637-5
Sunday at Home Crosswords	978-0-312-37834-3

Omnibus

Monday Crossword Puzzle Omnibus	978-1-250-02523-4
Tuesday Crossword Puzzle Omnibus	978-1-250-02526-5
Easy Crossword Puzzle Omnibus Volume 9	978-1-250-03258-4
Crossword Getaway	978-0-312-60824-8
Crosswords for Two	978-0-312-37830-0
Crosswords for a Weekend Getaway	978-0-312-35198-4
Crossword Puzzle Omnibus Vol. 16	978-0-312-36104-1
Sunday Crossword Omnibus Vol. 10	978-0-312-59006-2

Previous volumes also available

Portable Size Format

Relax and Unwind Crosswords	978-1-250-03254-6
Smart Sunday Crosswords	978-1-250-03253-9
Vacation for Your Mind Crosswords	978-1-250-03259-1
Crossword Diet	978-1-250-03252-2
Grab & Go Crosswords	978-1-250-03251-5
Colossal Crossword Challenge	978-1-250-03256-0
Holiday Crosswords	978-1-250-01539-6
Crafty Crosswords	978-1-250-01541-9
Homestyle Crosswords	978-1-250-01543-3
Picnic Blanket Crosswords	978-1-250-00391-1
Huge Book of Easy Crosswords	978-1-250-00399-7
Springtime Solving Crosswords	978-1-250-00400-0
Cunning Crosswords	978-0-312-64543-4
Little Book of Lots of Crosswords	978-0-312-64548-9
Effortlessly Easy Crossword Puzzles	978-0-312-64545-8
Big, Bad Book of Crosswords	978-0-312-58841-0
Midsummer Night's Crosswords	978-0-312-58842-7
Early Morning Crosswords	978-0-312-58840-3
Pop Culture Crosswords	978-0-312-59059-8
Mad Hatter Crosswords	978-0-312-58847-2
Crosswords to Unwind Your Mind	978-0-312-68135-7
Keep Calm and Crossword On	978-0-312-68141-8
Weekends with Will	978-0-312-65668-3
Every Day with Crosswords	978-0-312-65426-9
Clever Crosswords	978-0-312-65425-2
Everyday Easy Crosswords	978-0-312-64115-3
Poolside Puzzles	978-0-312-64114-6
Sunny Crosswords	978-0-312-61446-0
Mild Crosswords	978-0-312-64117-7
Mellow Crosswords	978-0-312-64118-4
Mischievous Crosswords	978-0-312-64119-1
Wake Up with Crosswords	978-0-312-60819-4
ABCs of Crosswords	978-1-250-00922-7
Best of Monday Crosswords	978-1-250-00926-5
Best of Tuesday Crosswords	978-1-250-00927-2
Dreaming of Crosswords	978-1-250-00930-2
Mad About Crosswords	978-1-250-00923-4
All the Crosswords that Are Fit to Print	978-1-250-00925-8
For the Love of Crosswords	978-1-250-02522-7
Sweet and Simple Crosswords	978-1-250-02525-8
Surrender to Sunday Crosswords	978-1-250-02524-1
Easiest Crosswords	978-1-250-02519-7
Will's Best	978-1-250-02531-9
Fast and Fresh Crosswords	978-1-250-02521-0

Other volumes also available

St. Martin's Griffin